THE
DEADLY TABLET

THE ABERMULE RAILWAY
DISASTER OF 1921

T0346798

THE
DEADLY TABLET

THE ABERMULE RAILWAY
DISASTER OF 1921

DAVID BURKHILL-HOWARTH

First published 2007

The History Press
97 St George's Place,
Cheltenham, Gloucestershire GL50 3QB
www.thehistorypress.co.uk

British Library Cataloguing in Publication Data.
A catalogue record for this book is available from the British Library.

ISBN 978 0 7524 4429 1

Typesetting and origination by The History Press
Printed by TJ Books Limited, Padstow, Cornwall

Contents

Acknowledgements

I am extremely grateful to the following people for their assistance; though this is with the usual proviso that any mistakes of omission, inclusion or interpretation are solely mine. In no particular order they are: Henry Wilson, for unlimited access to his vast collection of printed material on the Cambrian Railways; Margaret Stacy at Newtown Library, for her friendly and knowledgeable provision of local newspapers and material; Messrs Andrew Gardner and Mike Sparshot, signalmen on the Llangollen Railway, for imparting their knowledge of the operation of Tyer's No.6 machines, and letting me get my hands on one!; Terry Wain, headmaster of Abermule Primary School, for making available the material which was gathered for the seventy-fifth anniversary of the event; Rita Boswell, archivist at Harrow School, for information on former pupils who were killed or injured in the crash; Eva Bredsdorff, curator of the Powysland Museum, for providing the pictures taken to illustrate the complexity of the tablet system at the inquest; the 'guardians' of Dolhafren Cemetery, and Dallas Davies of Llanidloes, for help in finding the correct graves; the staff of the Cambrian Railway Society's museum at Oswestry; George Rogers, for his reminiscences about his father, Porter Ernest Rogers; Elvid Hardiman, for producing the excellent line drawings from my rough scribbles; Janet Joel, for unearthing material on James Shaw; Clive Edwards, of Tregynon for memorial finding and his father's photographs; Carl Jones, of Network Rail, for his comments on modern signalling and safety practices on the Cambrian; Mona Thomas, for her translations from the 'language of heaven'; Jonathan Williams, for picture research concerning his grandfather George Morris; David Owen Owen, for material on Captain Harold Owen Owen's life and family; Mrs A.E. Welsh, for providing an original copy of her father's poem about the crash; Colin Reed, for unearthing his collection of Abermule prints and postcards; Michael Freeman, curator, Ceredigion Museum, Aberystwyth, for unearthing material on the Shone family involvement in the crash. Also, to the many people who graciously gave of their time and knowledge after being prompted by the articles in the *County Times* and the BBC websites.

Brian Poole of Newtown must be especially thanked for so generously sharing his oral history research on Cambrian matters. His knowledge of the 'railway people' of the district has been invaluable; I only wish that I could have been of more help to him in return on his forthcoming work on Caersws. I highly commend his authoritative and very readable work on the Kerry Railway.

I am grateful to all the authors mentioned in the bibliography, for the background material and insights that they have provided, and also on occasion for their telling phrases, which I have borrowed because I could not better them.

And, not least, eternal thanks to my family for their help, encouragement and advice.

David Burkhill-Howarth
Tarvin, Cheshire, 2007

Introduction

This accident, which took place on the Cambrian Railways of mid-Wales in January 1921, is an excellent example of how even the most carefully devised systems and regulations can break down through hasty action and careless supervision. It also shows that no electrical or mechanical safety devices can totally eliminate the human element.

The portrayal of the sequence of events which led up to the accident is constrained by a number of influences. The events revolve around six people, two of whom died in the crash. Therefore, the main details of what occurred come from the memories of those who caused the event; these recollections must by their nature contain elements of self-justification and self-protection.

Naturally, the witness statements contradict each other; where this occurs I have made it clear and tried to give due weight and explanation to the individual statements; I have made any conjecture on my part quite clear. Finally, it must be remembered that the complete sequence of events took place within about ten minutes, on what had promised to be a very ordinary Wednesday at a sleepy Welsh country station.

The account, where possible, is taken from primary sources such as newspaper accounts, interviews and ministry reports. Where safe to do so, I have omitted some of the complexities of signal interlocking and single line working without detracting from the sequence of events. There comes a time when the research and correlation must come to an end, and the publication of findings to enlighten and encourage others must take place. Even though I am certain that there is more material 'out there', I offer the following study as a 'work in progress'. I would be very pleased to hear from anyone with comments or information, either about the technical or social aspects of the tragedy.

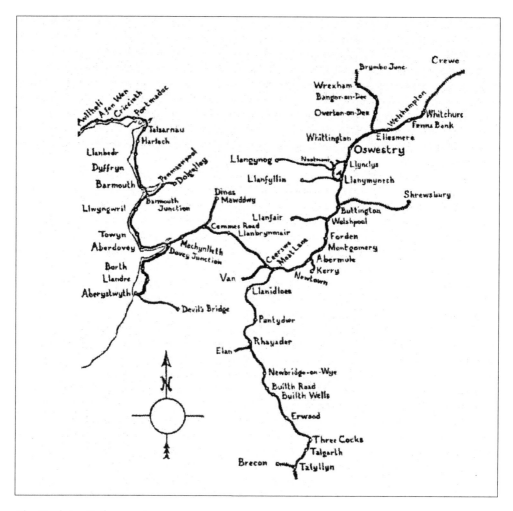

The Cambrian Railways system, *c.*1921.

The Cambrian Railways

The Cambrian Railways was the largest, though not the busiest, of the Welsh independent railway companies which opened up the principality in Victorian days. It came into being on 25 July 1864 when four small companies amalgamated. The joining of the Newtown, Machynlleth & Oswestry with the Llanidloes & Newtown, the Oswestry & Newtown and the Ellesmere & Whitchurch railways ended the isolation of many small villages and communities along the new company's 300 miles of branches and main lines. It delved into those parts of Wales where none of the other pre-grouping companies had found it worthwhile to extend.

The lines stretched from the English border, at Whitchurch, to the coast of Cardigan Bay between Pwllheli and Aberystwyth where they branched north and south, and through mid-Wales and the Wye Valley to Brecon. The connections to the north-west of England were via the London & North Western Railway (LNWR), whilst the Great Western Railway provided links for stations between London and North Wales.

Through the 1921 Railways Act, the 123 companies in existence at that time were merged into four large geographical groups. The Cambrian Railways company had always been most closely associated with the LNWR, but at the enforced grouping was merged into the GWR, a decision which was resented by many Cambrian men for years to come.

In 1866 the Cambrian headquarters moved from Welshpool to Oswestry. The original intention had been that Moat Lane Junction, geographically central to the operation, was to become the new headquarters. However, it was in the middle of nowhere, south of Newtown, and a large infrastructure would have been needed to support it. It was not until 1925, under GWR ownership, that a road was constructed from the rail junction to the main road about half a mile away. Eventually, there were sheds, exchange sidings, dozens of staff and a well-patronised refreshment room. The rather fine station which eventually ensued was demolished in 1965.

Oswestry developed rapidly because the Cambrian constructed its main works there to build and maintain its rolling stock, though it only ever built two locomotives of its own. The buildings and plant cost over £28,000 and through the Cambrian Railways' influence the town's population almost doubled within thirty years.

Because of the relatively small development of industry in mid-Wales, passenger services always formed the backbone of Cambrian traffic, yet that business was slow to develop partly because a number of opportunities were lost through directors falling out among themselves. The railway served only one large industrial town, Wrexham, and that was on a branch line.

The main line of the Cambrian Railways, from its junction with the LNWR at Whitchurch, through to the Welsh coast, was constructed with only single track for the majority of its length. This was done in order to get as much route mileage in place as rapidly as possible, with the least initial capital outlay being a contributing factor; the intention was to double it at a later date.

Although an Act of Parliament might have authorised the construction of a single-line section of a railway, the Board of Trade, recognising the inherent danger in such an operation, insisted on regarding the construction as incomplete. The railway company had to sign a Solemn Declaration under the company's seal; only one engine in steam should be permitted to enter any single-line section except where two or more engines formed a single train.

A Tyer's No.6 block instrument. This one is now at the Llangollen Railway.

The tablet instrument room at Abermule. The photograph was taken for Mr Warwick's evidence at the inquiry.

At the time in question there were four main lengths of single track, each with differing numbers of sections, and these were interspersed with double-track routes. The majority of the track remained single until the Cambrian was absorbed into the GWR in 1922.

The Whitchurch to Pwhelli main line was 132½ miles long with twelve important stations and thirty-four minor stations and conditional stops. At eight places connections with other lines or its own branches could cause delay; there were at least two sets of gradients which might call for another engine to assist. Between Whitchurch and Aberystwyth there were 247 over- and under-bridges, cattle creeps, stream/river crossings and the estuary bridges at Dyfi Junction and Borth. Because of these factors, schedules on the Cambrian were often more notional than real, and the employees struggled to keep the trains running on time. Unusually, and possibly uniquely on a British railway, the main line section – Aberystwyth to Whitchurch – ran for 95 miles with no tunnels.

Single-track
Operation

For a high proportion of the Cambrian Railways' mileage, trains ran in both directions over the same set of rails; this was potentially dangerous, but a very safe operating system had been developed over the years. Each single-line section, or block, of a few miles in length had a token which the engine driver had to have in his possession before he drove along it. This was done in addition to him obeying the signals. Every block had an instrument at each end containing the relevant tokens, and these were electrically connected in such a way that only one token could be obtained from either instrument at a time, no matter which way the train was running.

The equipment which made this possible was based on the 1878 patent of Edward Tyer; the two machines at Abermule were made under license by J.H. Saunders & Co. of Cardiff. The instruments, version No.6 by this time, were superbly constructed from solid machined brass and housed in large teak or mahogany boxes. Their sides were panelled, chamfered and moulded; their plungers, galvanometers and other external fittings were of brass or gun metal, whilst all screws were of brass. Everything fitted perfectly into the French-polished case. The whole thing was redolent of craftsmanship – but they were not easy to operate.

The signalmen sometimes called them 'chocolate machines' as they resembled the chocolate bar dispensers often seen on station platforms. A dozen or more tokens, or 'tablets' as they were called, were locked into each instrument to allow for uneven traffic working, so that trains could alternate, or follow in succession, in equal safety.

The tablets were circular metal discs about 4in in diameter and 1in thick. Each was embossed with the name of the section to which it belonged; in the centre of the disc was a shaped cut-out peculiar to that section. In the case of the sections in question, these were a square for Montgomery-Abermule and a circle for Abermule-Newtown. Once issued, the tablets were carried on the engine in a looped carrier with a leather pouch.

A second token could not be withdrawn at either end until the one already out was put back into one or other of the instruments. If a driver had a tablet for the section of line that he was on, it was a guarantee that no other tablet would be out and, therefore, no other train could be on the line whatever its direction of travel.

Thus the precautions were comprehensive and, for over thirty years since the installation of the system on the Cambrian, they had provided complete safety in traffic working.

Abermule looking towards Montgomery; the 'down' loop is in the centre and the Kerry branch is on the right.

Abermule Station looking towards Montgomery; taken from the Kerry branch lines towards the 'up' platform.

Abermule Station looking towards Newtown. The ground-frame is out of shot on the far right.

Abermule signal box and Kerry Road level-crossing gates.

Abermule
Station

To appreciate the circumstances which led to the terrible accident on Wednesday 26 January 1921, the station working in the upper Severn Valley needs to be considered. We start the investigation at Montgomery Station, which was actually situated 2 miles from the town of Montgomery. After 3½ miles in the 'down' direction, the line reached the crossing loop between the platforms at Abermule. The route then aimed westwards, 4 miles uphill towards Newtown, the next block station. Abermule was also the junction for the sleepy Kerry branch, but that played no part in the events.

The signal box was at the east end of the 'down' platform close to the Kerry Road level-crossings; this was the part of the station closest to Montgomery. The signal box contained twenty-two levers, seventeen for points and signals, one as the interlock for the six lever ground-frame and four spares – however, it contained neither tablet instruments nor level-crossing gate wheels.

The signalman had to go out to the lane to close the gates, or to the instrument room on the other platform to work the tablet instruments. The station building, such as it was, had been constructed on the opposite platform which catered for the 'up' trains. The tablet and telegraph instruments were in a special room leading out of the booking office. This arrangement had been inherited from the old telegraph system for 'space-interval' block working that had to be under the direct supervision of the stationmaster. The stations on either side of Abermule, however, did have their tablet instruments in the signal box.

At the Montgomery end of the station, the points leading to the passing loop – which formed the 'down' line and platform – were 155 yards from the signal box and worked from there, but at the Newtown end, the points were nearly 200 yards from the box and were worked from an interlocked mini-signal box known as a ground-frame. This was situated by the 'up' line at that end of the station. This ground-frame also controlled the Kerry branch's access to the main line, the goods wharf and the saw mills sidings. It was a major part of the traffic control system of the station, yet it was without direct contact with the signal box or telegraph/tablet room.

In the direction of Newtown, Abermule had a 'starter' signal and an 'advanced starter' to allow the shunting of wagons off the Kerry branch to take place within the station limits. The signalman in his box released the ground-frame's levers by reversing his interlocking lever, and a porter then set the points and operated the 'up' and 'down' line signals at the Newtown end of the station as required. The interlocking worked both ways. The signalman could pull his levers to operate his 'down' or 'up' signals at the Newtown end of the layout, but the arms would not drop to show clear unless the porter at the ground-frame had taken off his controlling lever. There was no direct link between the tablet machine, which gave permission to proceed and showed occupation of the line, and the locking of signals and points.

The booking office and waiting room on the 'up' platform. This block of buildings contained the telegraph/tablet room.

A small ground-frame similar to the one at Abermule.

'Down' advanced starter signal.

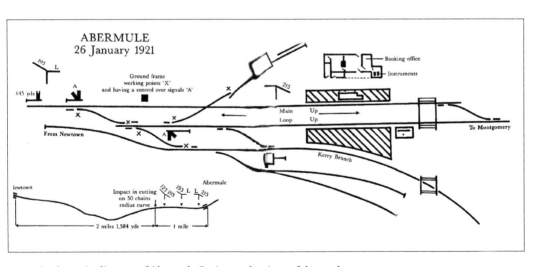

A schematic diagram of Abermule Station at the time of the crash.

A signal-box lever frame similar to that at Abermule; this picture was taken on the Llangollen Railway.

The Fateful Day

It was a cold but fine morning on the day in question; there was no rain, and visibility was good. At 10.53 a.m., a 'down' goods train left Abermule for Newtown, and the points at the Newtown end of the station were left in the 'loop to main' position after its departure. This was the first breach of operating rules.

The 10.05 a.m. 'all stations'-stopping passenger train from Whitchurch to Aberystwyth (expected there at 2.13 p.m.) was due at Abermule at 11.57 a.m., where it was scheduled to cross an 'up' train – the 10.25 a.m. Aberystwyth to Manchester express. By GWR or LNWR standards, 'express' was a courtesy title as the train was only booked at a 27–29mph average over the Cambrian sections. There were only two such crossings every twenty-four hours, the other being in the afternoon at 4.08 p.m.; the crossing was quite a big event in the station's day. However, the arrangement for the crossover was not rigidly enforced. If the stopping train was late it might be held for the express at Montgomery, but if it was running to time and the express was delayed, then Abermule might send it on to Newtown. In the previous sixty-four operating days, the crossover had occurred at Newtown on four occasions, and five times at Montgomery.

The staff at Abermule Station on that fateful day was as follows: relief-stationmaster Frank Lewis from Montgomery was deputising for the regular stationmaster, John Parry, who was on leave. Lewis was well acquainted with the routine at Abermule, having previously acted there on two or three other occasions as relief stationmaster and a similar number of times as signalman. Lewis, aged forty-seven, had served the Cambrian Railways for twenty-four years and had been a goods guard before qualifying as reliefman for minor stations in 1916. Although well known to the other members of staff, he was without doubt an outsider and considerably junior in service to the signalman, who was a possible choice to take charge in the regular stationmaster's absence. Lewis received £63 16s per annum.

Signalman William Thomas Jones (Bill) was sixty years old and had spent all his thirty-two-years' service at Abermule. Starting as a porter in 1888, he became a signalman-porter in 1891 and that was the job he was doing when we come across him, except that in 1918 he had been awarded the grade and pay of a signalman class 6. There had been a reduction of staff numbers and hours of working, and economies in general at Abermule during the previous two years. In spite of the Kerry branch, there was insufficient traffic to warrant a signalman who had no other responsibilities. Bill had been on duty since 3 a.m. with a one-hour break taken from 8.20 a.m.; this crossover was the last train movement of his shift. It is interesting to surmise that Bill Jones felt some hostility towards Lewis. Bill, as the 'old hand' on his home ground, probably felt that he was quite capable of looking after the station without the assistance of upstart ex-goods guards. No doubt the extra pay would have come in handy as well.

Also on the staff of the station that day was the booking clerk, Francis William Thompson of Llandyssil; he was a fifteen-year-old boy with two years' service. He was described at the inquest as being: 'a very intelligent lad and very sharp at school'. Ernie Percy Rogers of Garthmyl, who was seventeen with four years' service, was working as the station porter. One local source maintains that he had relatives working for the Cambrian, so this might have helped him obtain the post.

Not the actual people involved, but they are representative of the staff at Abermule.

Looking from the Kerry road, the stationmaster's house, where Lewis went for his meal, can be seen across from the signal box.

Neither of these youngsters was officially trained, nor permitted to take part in the operation of the signalling system. The stationmaster was not allowed to give them on-the-job training, though a semi-official blind-eye might have been turned to that if it had been done safely and conscientiously.

We must assume that Thompson and Rogers were both ordinary country lads who fancied a life with a modicum of excitement, a bit of a uniform and a small but steady wage, instead of being a farm hand or builder's labourer. They might have made it to signalman or stationmaster in the course of time.

The regular stationmaster, John Parry, had been in charge at Abermule for nearly four years and had left duty on 15 January for a fortnight's holiday. He was recalled to the station on 27 January.

The tragedy was due almost entirely to their combined carelessness and the lack of proper co-ordination in the execution of their respective duties. Only the stationmaster and the signalman were supposed to work the tablet instruments, but under Parry's acquiescence, it had become the practice for anyone who happened to be handy to operate them.

Bearing in mind the lack of proper organisation at Abermule, the fact that the Tyer electric-tablet instruments were installed in the station building and not in the signal box was most unfortunate.

Abermule Station was open for traffic movements between 3 a.m. and midnight. The movements averaged twenty-three per weekday, there being twenty-two such movements on Wednesdays, Fridays and Saturdays, and twenty-four on other weekdays. That year 26 January fell on a Wednesday and the booked movements were:

'Down' passenger trains	7	(Towards Newtown)
'Up' passenger trains	8	(Towards Montgomery)
(Eleven out of the fifteen passenger trains stopped at Abermule)		
'Down' goods trains	4	(Towards Newtown)
'Up' goods trains	3	(Towards Montgomery)

These movements were scheduled as follows:

Between	4 a.m. and 9 a.m.	5
	9 a.m. and Noon	5 (4) depending on cross-over
	Noon and 2 p.m.	0 (1) depending on cross-over
	2 p.m. and 8 p.m.	9
	8 p.m. and Midnight	3

Around 11.30 a.m. that morning, signalman Jones was in the instrument room on the 'up' platform, whilst Rogers and Thompson were in the booking office next door, having their lunch break. Relief-stationmaster Lewis had gone late for his dinner to the stationmaster's house, which was at the Montgomery end of the 'up' platform. The stationmaster usually took his lunch-break at 11.20 a.m. so as to be on hand to supervise the operation of the crossing movement, but on this day Lewis did not leave the station until 11.35 a.m. because of duties in the station yard. It was mooted locally at the time that part of his lunch might have been taken in the Waterloo Arms, although this was not brough out at the inquiry.

He was not present for the first part of the transactions over the line tablets, although back in 1919 special instructions had been sent out to all stationmasters that they must supervise the signalling personally and be present at the station when express trains were crossing on single-line sections.

The Trains are
Signalled

At 11.52 a.m., Signalman Seymour Humphreys at Montgomery Station 'asked the road' for the 10.05 a.m. ex-Whitchurch stopping train by sending 1-3-1 rings via his tablet instrument to Abermule. Jones accepted the train, and gave the necessary release for the Montgomery tablet machine by repeating the bell code and holding down the plunger on the last beat on the corresponding machine at Abermule. The Tyer's No.6 had electric indicators connected between the instruments at each end of the section. As a result of the signalmen's actions, the instruments at either end of the block now showed a red 'tablet out' indication for the 'down' train en route to Abermule.

The equivalent instrument for the 'up', Newtown-Abermule, section showed a white 'tablet in' indicator as no train was on the line. Thus a glance at the instruments was enough to show anyone the exact position of the line on either side of the station at any particular time.

Humphreys withdrew his tablet – No.18 Montgomery-Abermule – put it into its pouch and handed it to the driver of the train; he then pulled off his signals. The Whitchurch stopper set off four minutes late because of shunting by a previous goods train.

At 11.53 a.m. Humphreys sent two beats, the 'Train Entering Section' signal, to Jones at Abermule, who then telephoned Moat Lane Junction; this was situated 8½ miles south where the main line split either west to the coast or south to Brecon. Jones enquired as to the whereabouts of the Aberystwyth express and was told that the train was 'just leaving'.

The 'up' express was therefore 'right time', and Jones knew then that the express and the stopping train would definitely be crossing, as booked, at Abermule. According to some sources, he spoke to Humphreys over the telephone to tell him about this. On his way out through the booking office, Jones said to the two lads: 'The fast's off Moat Lane and the stopper's left Montgomery'.

As he went out on to the platform, signalman Jones claimed that he saw Frank Lewis, back from a short lunch, talking to a permanent-way inspector in the corner of the booking office; but he did not go and tell the stationmaster what the situation was. Jones said at the inquiry that he assumed that Lewis had heard the bells for the 'local', and would also deal with the express. However, it is apparent from the majority of the accounts that Lewis was not there at that time.

The stationmaster had been distracted from his normal schedule on returning from lunch by having to deal with the permanent-way sub-inspector, Thomas, who was enquiring about a wagon for loading wooden stakes on the following day. The matter of a wagon's availability was of some importance, as Thomas needed to travel onwards by the 'down' train. Lewis therefore went out with Thomas into the yard to see if a suitable wagon was available.

Thomas had arrived on the 10.17 a.m. goods, but after only a brief chat with Lewis had he gone to see the head 'ganger', who was working with his maintenance men about half a mile outside the station in the direction of Newtown. The 'ganger' was going to bring some wood up by rail trolley the following day and needed it loading into a wagon for Caersws. When Thomas arrived back at Abermule at about 11.30 a.m., Lewis was unloading sheets from a wagon in the yard with Signalman Jones. It is not recorded why Thomas did not go to him at that point.

Lewis then presumably went straight to his lunch, wherever it was taken, via the back of the station about 11.35 a.m. By 11.50 a.m. or so, the matter had suddenly become urgent and Thomas

Above: 'Asking the road' on the tablet machine for the 'local' from Montgomery.

Right: The original Tyer's No.6 block instrument for the 'up' direction at Abermule. The phone can be seen on the wall high up on the right.

Left: A well-known illustration, obviously posed, of a tablet being handed up to the footplate in its leather holder.

Below: Gangers at work on the Cambrian Railway; these ones were recorded passing by Machynlleth box.

put pressure on Lewis for a decision as soon as he returned from his break. Lewis did not go further than the wharf with Thomas, about 40-50 yards towards Newtown on the 'up' side; he expected to return in time to take the tablet from the 'down' train when it arrived, and replace it in the instrument. Next, he would collect the Newtown-Abermule tablet from the express and issue it with an Abermule-Montgomery token that he had just taken out after replacing the incoming 'down' tablet.

This tablet change-over with the express would have been done on the run with, under Cambrian regulations, two staff involved, one each to issue and to receive the tablets in their looped holders. However, at Abermule, normally it was only Parry who stood in the four-foot way to collect and issue the 'up' tablets; there is no record of how Lewis dealt with this important operation.

Finally, Lewis would also attend to the new tablet to be issued for the 'down' train to enable it to continue to Newtown after the express had passed through, though there was less urgency about this stage of the proceedings. One of the main complaints by passengers was the delay caused by the tablet change over when apparently nothing was happening to further their journey.

So far, apart from the signalman's discourtesy in not making sure that the stationmaster was kept up-to-date, everything was in order.

At 11.56 a.m., the bell on the Newtown-Abermule tablet instrument rang one beat. The young porter, Rogers, leaping up from the remains of his lunch next door, promptly answered it. He also acknowledged the four-bell code, which followed, requesting 'line clear' for the 'up' express. Rogers held down the plunger to send the electrical release to the Newtown instrument to unlock the tablet drawer. Lewis had, in all probability, just gone out of the yard door with inspector Thomas as the bell sounded. Rogers was not permitted to use the instrument and ought to have called Lewis in from the yard, or Jones from the box, but rules have rarely stopped a keen lad if he was enjoying himself.

Young Thompson was still with Rogers at this time, so he would have known what was happening with the express. His knowledge of the acceptance was never examined at the inquiry; he had a more serious part to play than this.

Rogers entered the time when he had released the tablet for the express in the train register that lay by the tablet machines. He then left the booking office to go to the ground-frame that was situated in a small shed at the Newtown end of the station yard; he was going to set the road for the express. There had been ample time to inform Lewis or Jones of his action in accepting the express – by any account, at least one of them was within shouting distance. But he did not do so.

Everything was still technically in order; the two trains were approaching Abermule from opposite directions, each bearing the correct tablet for the section it occupied – whilst both the tablet instruments at Abermule were now automatically locked so that no other tablet could be withdrawn. They clearly showed this state of affairs on the indicators.

Operating the ground-frame was Rogers' usual and permitted duty, and about three minutes would have been occupied in reaching his post. It may be assumed, therefore, that he arrived at the ground-frame at 12 p.m., or just after. On his arrival, he found that the points at the Newtown end of the station were still set for the 'down' road after the previous goods train; when he tried to alter their position he was unable to reverse the lever. Had he called on signalman Jones at this stage to release the lock so that he could re-set the points to the 'up' platform, Jones would have realised that the express was approaching Abermule. The signalman knew from his telephone inquiry to Moat Lane that the express was running to time, but only Rogers knew positively that the express had been permitted to occupy the Newtown-Abermule section.

Train register and warning flags.

Jones, meanwhile, had closed the crossing gates to road traffic, then gone into the signal box and lowered the 'down' home signal for the 'local' train to enter the station. According to the report of the official inquiry, the setting of this signal to 'clear', when the train was not in sight, was a breach of block working. It should not have been cleared until the train was brought to a halt and only then should it have been lowered to allow the train to draw into the station. Present-day signalman Sparshot of the Llangollen Railway, where similar practices are still in operation, believes Jones was correct in his action. There was, however, still a potentially dangerous situation because the points at the Newtown end of the station lay set for the 'down' loop line with the incoming express expected shortly.

At 12.02 p.m., five minutes late, the 'down' train arrived, and Jones then replaced the 'home' signal to danger, and went out of the signal box on to the 'down' platform. Presumably, the gates remained closed to road traffic; the train may even have been fouling the crossing.

In the published timetable, only the time of the 'local's arrival was given. The *Working Time Book* issued to the staff, however, gave both the time of arrival and departure. This was done in order to get the 'local' into Abermule with plenty of time to organise the tablet change, and the resetting of the points. The tablet change sometimes caused delay, and the staff were hauled over the coals if this occurred.

There was a suggestion at the time that Jones was keen to be on the platform when the stopper arrived in case there were any tips to be had from helping alighting passengers with their luggage. Laughter ran round the court when Jones was questioned on this matter at the inquest;

it was the only time that there was any lightness in the dire proceedings. The coroner suggested that his signalling duties should have taken precedence. Jones presumably returned to his box more or less immediately as passenger numbers were low on that trip.

Meanwhile, after leaving the tablet room, Thompson had gone to the foot crossing at the Montgomery end of the station so that he could savour the fun of having the engine pass within inches of his nose as he took the tablet from the firemen of the incoming train. Thompson knew that it was the duty of the signalman or stationmaster to do this, but as Lewis was not there, and Jones was in the signal box, he collected the tablet holder as he had done on other occasions under Parry's tenure. No doubt he thoroughly enjoyed the experience.

At the inquiry, Thompson also stated that he had been instructed more than once by signalman Jones to get a tablet out of an instrument. This was apparently to save Jones the trouble of crossing to the 'up' platform and doing it himself. In the words of the coroner, Thompson was the 'sort of lad who was ready to oblige the stationmaster or signalman if they felt disinclined to move about.' Rogers, too, was apparently encouraged to act well above his authority and capability in order to save his superiors' legs. He also helped the Kerry branch guard to carry out shunting operations.

There is no doubt that, for all the slipshod methods that were prevalent at Abermule, the intentions of the two youths were honourable enough; they wanted to keep the traffic moving, whilst enjoying themselves. As with all single-line railways, there were long periods of calm on the Cambrian main line, followed by intense activity for a few minutes as trains crossed, after which everything lapsed into calm again. The crossing of the 10.05 a.m. from Whitchurch and the 10.25 a.m. from Aberystwyth at Abermule was such a period of intense activity.

Thompson returned to the 'up' platform with the tablet holder, and went into the booking hall with the intention of going through into the instrument room to place the tablet in the Montgomery-Abermule instrument. It transpired at the inquest that he had probably done this nearly 100 times since starting work at Abermule.

Lewis' attention had been called to the 'down' train by the noise of its arrival, so he ran back to the booking office via the yard door. As he entered the booking hall, he met Thompson coming off the platform. Unbeknown to anyone involved, this was the pivotal moment of the whole affair.

The young lad, knowing that he was not permitted to handle the tablet, thrust it guiltily into Lewis' hands saying, 'Change this tablet, Frank. I'll go and see to the tickets'. Lewis later swore that Thompson had said, 'Take this tablet to the 'down' train, Frank. They're going on.' Lewis claimed that Thompson was coming from the tablet room.

The two statements are at variance one with another. Each person stuck firmly to his own account, and though probably neither statement is entirely correct, it seems that Lewis's variation is the least likely to be accurate.

If, instead of taking the word of a boy of fifteen, a lad, moreover, with an impediment in his speech, the stationmaster had looked at his instruments, or at the tablet in his hand, he would have seen the true situation. This was that the instrument for the Newtown-Abermule section had a tablet out for the 'up' express, and that the tablet he was holding, and was expecting to give to the 'local' crew as a token of safe passage to Newtown, was for the 'down' section, Montgomery-Abermule.

Following on from whatever was first said, both participants agreed that Lewis then asked Thompson, 'Where's the 'up' fast?' To which Thompson replied vaguely, 'About Moat Lane'. This was most misleading because the train had actually passed Moat Lane about ten minutes earlier, and was at that moment leaving Newtown under clear signals with a tablet authorising it to proceed to Abermule.

Why Thompson should have said this when he knew from signalman Jones that the express had long ago passed Moat Lane must be put down to Thompson's youth and fluster at being caught out with the tablet. Thompson had also heard Rogers accept the express from Newtown even more recently; confusingly, Rogers later claimed that Thompson had left the tablet room before him to go and stand on the 'up' platform, waiting for the express.

Lewis had already assumed that Thompson had replaced the Montgomery-Abermule tablet, and issued an Abermule-Newtown one; he now believed that the express was behind time.

In the stationmaster's account of the incident, it was implied that the crossing of the two trains was not going to take place at Abermule, but that the stopping train was to go on to Newtown because the express was apparently running late. This alteration could have been made legally under the authority of the signalman; according to some parties it was not unusual for this to occur, though Parry, the stationmaster, later claimed that this happened very rarely.

Lewis thought that the tablet he now held in his hand authorised the train in the station to proceed towards Newtown. In fact, it would have been impossible to obtain such a tablet because the Abermule-Newtown instrument had been locked through Rogers' previous action in accepting the express. Sadly, he did not check that.

It might be imagined that if a train arrived at Abermule from Newtown, and there was a train at Abermule waiting to go to Newtown, surely all that had to be done was to take the tablet from the driver of the Newtown train, and give it to the man who was going in the reverse direction. This was possible, but illegal because it would lead to slackness in working; more importantly, it would not enable the indicators on the tablet instruments to register the correct situations.

Only if the tablet from the arriving 'up' train was placed in the instrument, and both indicators on the section restored so that they showed the tablet for the 'up' train was in, could the second set of operations, the issue of a 'down' tablet for the same section of line, legitimately be carried through. This was the sole way in which the indicators would correctly show, for the next train movement, that a tablet was out for a train running in the 'down' direction.

During the flurry and excitement of the local's arrival, a bell signal had been sent from Newtown by station-foreman Brock at 11.59 a.m., when the express left his station after a two-minute stop. It came out at the inquiry that it was not unusual for this bell signal to be sent before the express had even stopped at Newtown; another example of sloppy working on the Cambrian. However, on this occasion, though sent correctly, the signal was not answered from Abermule, and there was no relative entry in the Train Register sat alongside the instruments. Brock repeated the advice several times, with no acknowledgement.

It is, therefore, clear that there was no one in the booking office or instrument room at Abermule when this bell signal sounded, and no one was aware that the express had actually left Newtown.

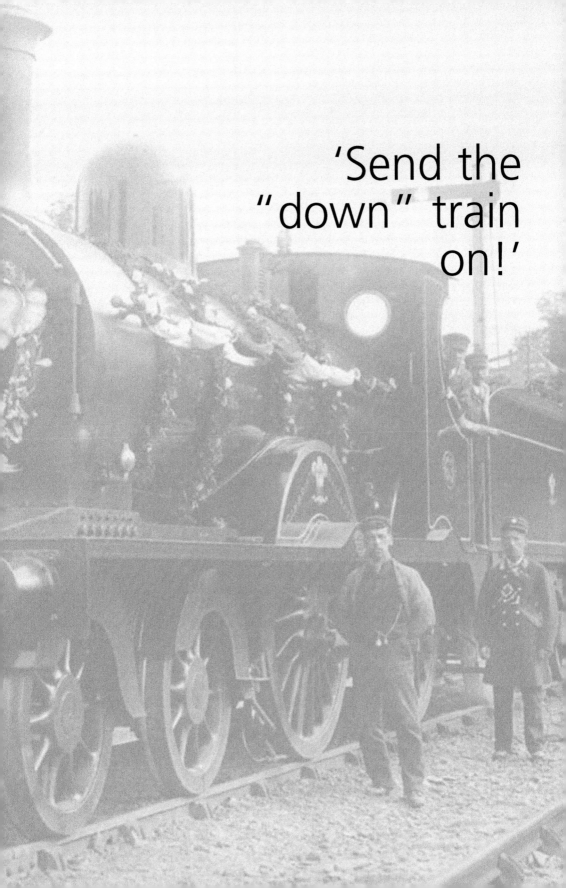

'Send the
"down" train
on!'

With over twenty-years' experience, Lewis took the word of the confused boy and assumed that the controller at Moat Lane had altered the usual crossing arrangements. He knew that the margin of time was now small for the 'down' train to reach Newtown and clear the road without delaying the express. All of a sudden, the tempo had picked up.

Lewis told Thompson to go to the signal box and tell Jones to pull off his signals for the 'down' train. The signalman was not allowed to lower the signals until he had been authorised to do so by the man issuing the tablet. Some of the larger or busier stations had official messenger boys for this very purpose; this was not the case at Abermule. Nor, it transpired at the inquest, had Thompson ever relayed a message of such importance before.

Jones said that Thompson came every day to give him the message about going on. He later said that Parry usually came to give him instructions; this was the first time that the lad had brought such a message. Thompson had given him messages, but not regarding sending the 'local' on in preference to waiting for the express.

Confusingly, Thompson said that he never saw Jones at that time. The lad also claimed that he did not see what the stationmaster did after he had handed him the tablet holder.

As Thompson ran one way along the 'up' platform towards the signal box, Lewis ran the other way. He crossed the 'up' road to where the engine of the 'local' train was standing at the 'down' platform. He handed the tablet in its pouch to fireman Evans; without troubling to examine it, Evans then placed it in his cab. Under the company's regulations, Rule 31, whoever took the tablet from the instrument was responsible for handing it to the driver – there was to be no intermediary.

Like the stationmaster, the fireman took the system for granted also. For years the Tyer electric-block system had protected the line infallibly and he conceived no reason for, or possibility of, error.

Driver Jones did not see the handover for he was going round his engine with the oil-can as was the practice of old-time drivers whenever they got the chance. Under working rules it was the driver's duty to examine the tablet and ensure that it was correct before hanging it up in the cab, but he failed to do so. There are suggestions that a regrettable 'etiquette' had developed around the tablet handover, where to actually examine a tablet was to imply mistrust in the station staff. Obviously there is no record of this, but Henry Warwick in his evidence as superintendent of the line, agreed that 'the tendency would be by practice to assume that it would be the right one, knowing that other people must have failed if it were the wrong one.' The guard should have also been shown the tablet by the stationmaster before he handed it to the footplate crew, though there was no requirement for the guard to examine it and the display was often done from a distance.

At the inquest, guard Chetwood, who appeared badly shaken and complained of deafness after the accident, said that he did not see who it was that handed the tablet to the engine crew. If either the driver or the fireman had examined the tablet before the train started from Abermule, they would have seen that it was the tablet that they had just brought from Montgomery. No doubt there would have been some very severe words and some local repercussions, but the incident would have stopped at that point. Abermule would never have been famous in the annals of railway history.

As we have seen, there was no obvious explanation for that serious omission of examining the tablet, except perhaps that the crew had been thrown out of their routine. They were no longer to wait peacefully for the express to go through, but were suddenly expected to get to Newtown to clear the road; compounding the problem, they had arrived late at Abermule, cutting into their available time to do that. Lewis had startled the crew by his sudden, hurried appearance clutching a tablet holder when none was expected and all of a sudden they were on their mettle to keep the company's 'crack' express running to time.

Thompson, meanwhile, had collected the ticket of the one passenger who had alighted from the 'down' train and, at some stage, he took various letters and parcels off the guard. Thompson must have assumed that the stationmaster had changed the tablet whilst he, Thompson, was dashing around, if, indeed, the lad ever thought about it at all.

Although the circumstances were now extremely dangerous, there was still one last possibility that disaster could be averted. If anyone had looked at the indicators on the Tyer's instruments they would have seen that there was a tablet out for a 'down' train between Montgomery and Abermule, the train actually standing in the station, and a tablet was out for an 'up' train between Newtown and Abermule. Yet here was the 'down' train about to leave Abermule for Newtown.

No one had been in the tablet room at all since Rogers had accepted the 'up' express from Newtown. The arrival of the 'down' train had been completely unrecorded, so far as tablet instruments or the Train Register were concerned. Montgomery did not even know that the 'local' had arrived at Abermule.

Rogers, at the ground-frame, was now in charge of over half of the station's traffic regulating capacity, yet this was only permitted under the strict supervision of the stationmaster. The young porter was the only person who had taken any part in the handling of the 'up' express, and he had not told anyone that he had accepted it and enabled the issue of a tablet to its driver at Newtown. His unauthorised action in accepting the train was more the result of lax supervision and operating practices, than any fault of his own.

Rogers had correctly expected that signalman Jones or stationmaster Lewis, after the arrival of the 'down' train, would go over to the instrument room to replace the incoming tablet, thus notifying Montgomery of the train's arrival at Abermule.

Whoever did it, they would then have obtained a token for the express to run to Montgomery; when doing so he would have seen that the express was on its way to Abermule by the status of the other instrument. Neither of them had done any of that.

Rogers had also expected that Thompson would receive and book the 'train entering section' bell signal for the express that Rogers had accepted, on its receipt from Newtown. The lad should then have informed the rest of the staff that the express was on its way. Thompson, however, had dashed off, leaving the office unmanned, so that he could collect the token from the 'down' train.

Rogers, after much indecision at the ground-frame, went out on to the 'up' road to shout to the signalman to release the lever in the signal box that would free the ground-frame and allow him to set the points to the 'up' road for the express. The points lever was locked for the loop by the 'down' starting signal at the end of the platform, which Jones had pulled off in accordance with Lewis' instructions, if not well before receiving them. The guard of the 'local', Chetwood, gave evidence at the inquest that both the 'down' starter and the advanced starter signals were off as the train arrived in the station. This meant that nothing had been put to danger since the goods had left nearly an hour earlier.

Rogers did not apparently notice the position of the starter signal, even though it was in his line of sight as he looked towards the signal box. As noted earlier, there was no

From this spot, Rogers was now in charge of over half of the station's traffic regulating capacity.

interlock mechanism between the starting signal and the Montgomery-Abermule tablet instrument.

The porter then noticed the stationmaster standing in the 4ft way between the tracks, by the engine, signaling with his hand 'right away' to the train crew. Lewis, contrary to Chetwood's evidence, remembered the starter signal being at clear, and the advanced starter being 'on' at danger. The engine whistle was sounded by the fireman to acknowledge the 'right away', and calling for the advanced starting signal to be lowered by Rogers. Rogers could draw only one conclusion. It was that someone in authority had cancelled the acceptance of the 'up' express and the tablet, whose release he had authorized, had been replaced in the Newtown instrument.

So he returned to the ground-frame and pulled over the lever working the 'down' advance-starting signal. The road was now set for the train to proceed towards Newtown; the 'local' set off on its way at 12.03 p.m.

The train had been stopped in the station for less than two minutes according to its guard, and also the operating manager of the line, who happened to be on the train. Once past the advanced starter, the train was technically outside the station boundaries, and under the protection, or in this case, otherwise, of the block system.

A Cambrian Railway's 4-4-0 locomotive similar to the ones involved in the crash; this one is dressed for a Royal train. The guard is Edward Shone who died at Abermule.

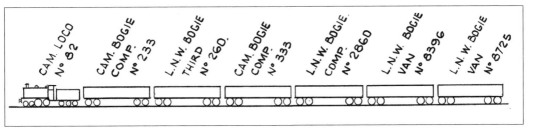

The composition of the 'down' local.

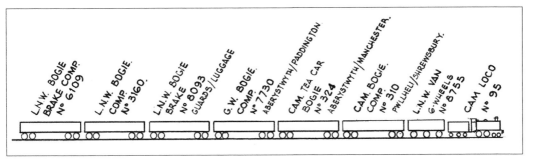

The composition of the 'up' express.

Sub-inspector Thomas had managed to catch the train; riding in the guard's van he was happy in the knowledge that his ganger's wagon was sorted for the morrow, but ignorant of the small part he had played in the coming tragedy.

The 'local' and the express that was rapidly coming towards it, were each hauled by a Cambrian 4-4-0 passenger locomotive with six-wheeled tender, resplendent in black paint lined with gamboge and edged with vermillion. The express engine would have had the company coat-of-arms displayed on its sides.

Engine No.82 of Class 21, a so-called 'Large Sharp', after its maker, Sharp Stewart of Glasgow, was on the 'down' stopping train; it had a load of six eight-wheeled coaches; a mix of Cambrian and LNWR stock as follows:

Cambrian composite (1st & 3rd compartments) coach 233
LNWR 3rd class 260
Cambrian composite coach 333
LNWR composite coach 2860
LNWR brake 8396
LNWR brake 8725.

The express was hauled by engine No.95, one of the largest engines on the line; its train consisted of six eight-wheeled coaches marshalled behind a six-wheeled goods van as follows:

An LNWR six-wheeled goods van, 8755
Cambrian corridor coach, 310, Pwllheli to Shrewsbury;
Cambrian corridor coach, 324, Aberystwyth to Manchester with buffet at the front
GWR coach, 7730, Aberystwyth to Paddington with guard's brake section
LNWR guards/luggage van, 8093
LNWR coaches, 3160 and 6109

Because of the multiplicity of coaches belonging to other companies that were marshalled in its trains, the Cambrian was a great user of roof-boards on its coaches, showing their departure and destination stations. Both trains were fitted with Gresham & Craven continuous vacuum brakes, working blocks on the engine and tender wheels, and on all the wheels of the coaching vehicles, except the centre pair of van No.8755 on the express.

Disaster is
Imminent

At about 12.03 p.m., just as the 'down' train was starting, Thompson, the fifteen-year-old clerk, went into the tablet room to give the 'train entering section' signal to Newtown, and, belatedly, 'train out of section' to Montgomery; once again helpful, but not his job. It was not until this young boy looked at the instruments that anyone realised the terrible mistake that had been made.

As Frank Lewis too walked back into the instrument room intending to send 'train entering section' to Newtown for the slow train he saw the instrument's indicator and his blood must have frozen in his veins. The Newtown-Abermule tablet instrument already had its red 'tablet out' indicator showing. That could only mean that Newtown had withdrawn a tablet for the express, unless some other member of his staff had just sent the 'train on line' bell.

He knew that this was impossible because none of them had had a chance to do it. However, clutching desperately at straws, he telephoned Newtown and asked: 'Has the "up" fast left you yet?' To which James Brock, acting as signalman at East Cabin, Newtown, replied, 'I put it on to you six minutes ago.' Brock then heard Lewis say, 'Good God! And the "down" train has gone.'

Lewis ran out of the office and on to the platform yelling to Bill Jones that the 'down' train had gone to Newtown with the wrong tablet. Brock was left shouting down the phone line to an empty tablet room, 4 miles away from him.

The train was already out of sight thanks to Lewis' delay in facing facts. Jones tried to attract the driver's attention by wagging the arm of the 'up' distant signal, about three-quarters of a mile towards Newtown, but the train was already beyond the signal, and indeed beyond all help. Although an accident was now inevitable, and the crash that happened was bad enough in all conscience, it might have been much worse had not the enginemen of the express been as diligent and alert as the men on the 'down' stopping train were negligent.

George Jones driving the 'local' was the oldest driver on the district, having completed half a century on the railway; he was one of the regular Royal Train drivers on the Cambrian. He lived at 9 Hafren Terrace, Llanidloes, and was the treasurer of the local branch of the NUR. He would have been off shift in about twenty minutes when his train arrived at Moat Lane Junction.

Albert Evans, his fireman, from the same village, had fought in France. Whilst he was on the Western Front in 1917, he had been severely gassed and left for dead. After a lengthy stay in hospital and protracted convalescence, he had been discharged and returned to the Cambrian. The guard of the 'local' train reported at the inquest that both members of the engine's crew were in good health on that January morning.

The reason for the 'local' crew not keeping a good look out was never examined at the inquest or the official inquiry because they were both killed in the crash. It might be conjectured that, in fact, the fireman was not in such good health as he led outsiders to believe and his driver was taking a 'turn on the shovel' to give him a break on what they thought was a clear line.

The express train from Newtown was driven by John Pritchard Jones; passed-fireman Albert Owen was on the footplate with him. The status of 'passed-fireman' meant that he had been examined and was authorised to drive as well as stoke the boiler.

Above: Driver George Jones; possibly the most experienced driver on the district.

Right: Fireman Albert 'Penri' Evans. He was buried with his wife and child at Rhayader.

The clear and open view from the local's footplate looking towards Newtown. The overbridge is just round the bend.

The restricted view from the Express' footplate at the overbridge.

The Crash

The inevitable collision occurred at a point one mile south-west of Abermule Station, close to a place called Red House Crossing. The railway from Abermule leading to this point was on a low-rising embankment and there was nothing to obstruct the 'local' crew's view of the line. There were a number of indications of where they were at any one time. There were two 'cattle creeps' under the tracks shortly after leaving Abermule. Then there was a 'down' stop signal, about 200 yards before the over-bridge, operated by the farmer at Cilgwrgan if he needed to move vehicles or livestock across the railway. There appeared to be no corresponding signal in the 'up' direction, presumably the line of sight was sufficient. As was common on the Cambrian in such circumstances, neither was there a 'down distant' signal as a warning of a possibly adverse signal; however, the 'home' was set well back from the crossing. This was another reason why the 'local' crew should have been keeping watch out at this point. They should have also been keeping a lookout for sub-inspector Thomas' gang which was somewhere about that point. The ganger was not called to give evidence at the inquiry.

Newtown is 4 miles from Abermule, and the express had accelerated in good style. It was running at about 45-50mph when it reached the usual point for shutting off steam prior to slowing down for the tablet exchange at Abermule.

Drivers on 'up' trains normally closed the regulator somewhere near the level-crossing known as Cilgwrgan, close to the quaint black-and-white farm of the same name; it was about three-quarters of a mile from an occupation bridge, No.148, over the railway. This bridge was built in the early years of the century as a result of incidents at a previously unguarded level-crossing there.

The express passed under the bridge on a short length of right-hand curve – this lay in a cutting whose slopes fell in height from about 16ft at the over-bridge to 3ft at the site of the accident. It was possibly the only place on the whole main line where the view was so restricted. The fireman of the express rode on the left-hand side of the footplate and the driver on the right; fireman Owen's view from the left, although it was on the outside of the curve, was obstructed by the boiler of the engine.

Driver Pritchard Jones appears to have been a conscientious type. He had personally inspected and accepted the token at Newtown when most drivers left the job to their firemen. He was also keeping a sharp look out between signals, as well as riding with his hand on the brake. As soon as he passed under the bridge, he saw the smoke of the 'local' – it was about 350 yards distant – no more. Almost instantly Pritchard Jones braked his train as hard as he could – the smoke could only mean one thing. He just had time to wind the steam cut-off valve into reverse. Retired driver 'Abergynolwyn' Davies has commented, however, that unless Pritchard Jones also had time to reopen the regulator to allow steam through the reverser it would have had little effect on slowing down the train.

The combined speed of the two trains at impact would have been about 60mph, approximately 30 yards per second, so, depending on the efficiency of the braking there would have been only 10-12 seconds before they crashed. According again to driver Davies, the vacuum brakes were good but not particularly fast acting.

An interview given to the *Daily Sketch* reporter by driver Pritchard Jones, whilst he was still in hospital, suggests that he saw his fireman 'with his hand firmly on the brake', though this was not mentioned in the official depositions by either man. Pritchard Jones was still rather confused at that time as not many hours had passed since the accident, and he had suffered severe blood loss. It was during this interview that he realised that the other crew had died.

The crew of the 'down' train did not appear to see the express because the column of smoke continued to pillar skywards as their engine laboured hard against the rising grade. The driver of the express claimed that he never whistled; his priority was to reduce his train's speed. However, witnesses, including his fireman, heard a whistle just before the collision. Did the driver of the 'local' catch sight of the express bearing down on him at the last minute and take some belated action? In support of this, Owen clearly saw smoke and steam coming from the 'local' when he first sighted it, but he thought as he jumped that the steam had been shut off.

The guard of the 'local', Edwin Chetwood, who was riding in the last vehicle but one, an LNWR brake van, reported to the inquiry that to his knowledge the continuous vacuum brake had not been applied. John George, the chief traffic inspector of the Cambrian, who was riding in the train, also gave expert evidence which corroborated this. There was no possibility of determining the state of the braking system from the remains of the wrecked engine.

After the dreadful Irish rail accident at Armagh in 1889, a law was passed making automatic and continuous brakes – either vacuum or compressed air – compulsory on all passenger trains in the United Kingdom; nearly all the companies adopted the vacuum brake. Gresham & Craven's standard vacuum brake had been awarded a Gold Medal at the Paris Exhibition in 1888 and became almost universally the unit of choice.

There might have been a small chance of averting the disaster if both trains had braked immediately, certainly the impact would have been greatly lessened if either member of the Whitchurch crew had spotted the express and taken some action. However, the Cambrian's chief engineer and locomotive superintendent, George McDonald, was emphatic at the inquest that there had been no possibility of the two trains stopping in time, even if both crews had braked immediately.

Driver Pritchard Jones and fireman Owen had stepped outside of their cab and were riding on the footsteps knowing that they had done all they could. The towering column of smoke from the 'local' came ever closer. They hung on until the very last second, and then jumped clear. They were almost immediately buried under a hail of wood and metal as the trains met and shattered. Both men were knocked unconscious briefly, as well as being injured to varying degrees.

The brakes of the express train had bit hard against the wheels, but not hard enough to save the situation; the 254-ton express was running on a falling gradient of 1:123, still making about 25-30mph when it rammed head-on into the 217-ton 'local' train, labouring hard at about the same speed.

The crash occurred at approximately 12.06 a.m.

The inevitable happened at approximately 12.06 p.m.

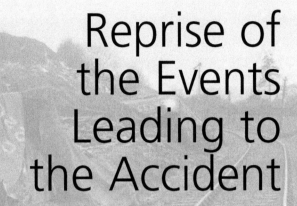

Reprise of
the Events
Leading to
the Accident

We may take it as certain that the errors committed at Abermule Station on 26 January 1921 were by no means unique on the Cambrian, or any other railway. At many another single-line crossing station, unauthorized staff had worked the tablet instruments or had passed the safety tokens from hand-to-hand, bypassing those instruments. Other stationmasters had, for one reason or another, failed to be present at the arrival of a train and then authorized the 'right away' without proper assurance that all was as it should be. Many a driver had received a tablet authorising him to proceed and had not examined it. Time and again mistakes had been made with impunity on the Cambrian; signalman John Evans at Talerddig was censured three years on the run for irregularities in tablet operation, yet somehow he retained his job.

However, at Abermule on that disastrous day, those errors joined one another until the outcome was certain. Ironically, it did not help that the system was well-tried and apparently foolproof. Rail travel had become a lot safer around the turn of the century. The last passenger train collision on a single track in the United Kingdom to result in fatalities had been at Radstock on 7 August 1876, over forty-four years previously.

In view of the company's explicit instructions to stationmasters to give personal attention to the crossing of the two trains, the first mistake relief-stationmaster Lewis made on this particular day was in taking his dinner later than usual, although this was caused by attending to company business. As a result, he did not return to the station building until ten minutes after the usual time, and uncomfortably close to the expected arrival of the 'local' that was to halt at Abermule to let the express pass.

His second mistake was to immediately leave the office on another company errand without first finding out where the express was and without arranging to be called as soon as it was 'belled'. The accident would never have occurred if he had been told on his return from lunch that the express was already well past Moat Lane Junction.

Lewis acknowledged full responsibility for his failure to examine the tablet. He also agreed that he had made no alteration in the station's working practices when he took over as relief, although he could see that they did not conform to company rules and regulations. For instance, it was common for the young booking clerk, Thompson, to be unlawfully involved in the tablet changing, but he, Lewis, had merely cautioned him to be careful.

It can be supposed that this lack of 'pulling the staff up by their boot-laces' might, in part, have been because of a strained relationship with signalman Jones, the old hand on the station. Knowing that he was only there for a short period, it was presumably easier for Lewis to work with the Abermule system of operating a railway than the Cambrian's. Jones, from what can be deduced from this incident, did not attempt to assist, or coordinate his knowledge of a situation with the stationmaster.

Jones appeared to consider himself entirely free from blame in the event. Yet, it was his duty, in the absence of the stationmaster, to receive the tablet from the 'down' train, and, if he had performed that duty on that day, the accident would not have happened.

He knew well in advance that the express had passed Moat Lane Junction on time, but made no attempt to pass on the information to Lewis. Moreover, if – as he claimed – Lewis was within earshot of the phone conversation, neither did he make any attempt to check if Lewis had registered the information. Jones did not subsequently take any action to find out what had happened to the express when the crossing plans were changed, though he knew that unless a breakdown had occurred, it should pass the 'down' train at Abermule as planned. Although he was absent on the day, Parry, the regular stationmaster, was responsible for allowing the development of irregular operating practices in the custody and transference of tablets. He claimed that he never authorised clerk Thompson or porter Rogers to use the instruments, but maintained that they were to call him if there were any bell signals.

Rogers was permitted to work the tablet instruments only under Lewis' direct supervision as an unofficial trainee, but Thompson had no authority to touch the machines at all. However, both the boys' signatures appeared in the Train Register. Parry had occasionally signed the Train Register as if he had carried out the duty when in fact he had been elsewhere on the station premises.

Members of the Cambrian traffic staff, in particular Inspector Ellis Lloyd, were not completely blameless either in this unauthorised working; managers must have been able to feel a sense of what was going on at the station by the entries in the Train Register, which they were supposed to check regularly.

The crew of the 'local' train from Whitchurch, through lack of attention at the station and on the track, for whatever reason, held at least half the responsibility for the crash. Between them all, they caused a significant number of deaths and injuries of Cambrian passengers and employees through their slap-happy working and, perhaps, a little bit of resentment or an uneasy working relationship.

The only operating staff immediately involved who came well out of the event were the driver and fireman of the Aberystwyth express, who did everything they could to mitigate the disaster – they only had a few brief moments after sighting the 'local' steaming hard towards them on the same line.

A view of the crash after the line was re-opened. The small white post in the distance, to the right of the track, marks the impact point.

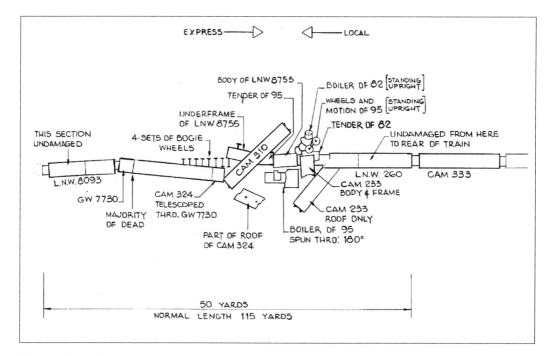

Diagram of wreckage.

Right at the heart of the crash.

'Like a matchbox tray slammed into its cover.' This appears to have been taken after the first frantic rescue attempts had been completed.

A similar view to the previous one, showing the smallholdings under construction in the background.

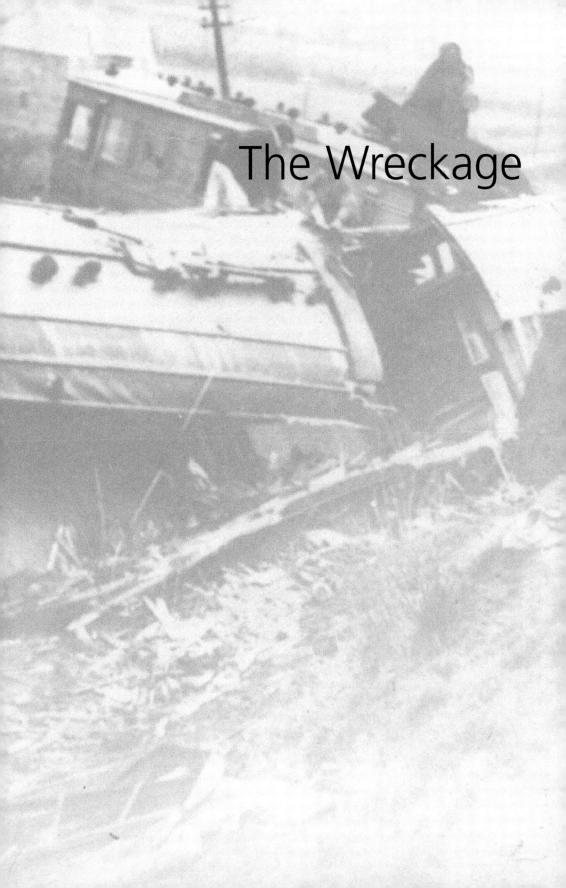

The Wreckage

In the silence of the early twentieth-century countryside, the collision at Red House Crossing was heard many miles away. The four men standing on the platform at Abermule were left in ignorance no longer as to the consequences of their incompetence, over-enthusiasm, and slack working practices. No doubt they were too shaken to take any further part in the subsequent rescue operation. The local paper reported one of them as saying: 'We knew what was going to happen; we were waiting to be told where it happened.'

Foreman Brock at Newtown possibly also heard the crash; he too must have been expecting it, and no doubt sent the dreaded 'six bells – obstruction danger', to Moat Lane in the rear. Hopefully, Jones at Abermule had the presence of mind to send the same signal to Montgomery.

The total length of both trains was 252 yards before the crash; afterwards, the wreckage covered a line about 160 yards long. The two engines, tenders and five coaches (four of the express and one of the slow train), which normally occupied a space of about 115 yards, formed a tangled mass of wreckage only about 50 yards long. Fortunately, the rear four coaches of the 'local' and the rear three coaches of the express remained on the rails – the end ones were little damaged, except for distorted buffers.

The boiler of the express engine, No.95, had been wrenched from its frame, spun round and had hit the ballast facing the way it had come, lying south of the track; the running gear of the engine stood vertically over the rails. Its tender was later repaired, and returned to service.

The frame of LNWR six-wheeled parcel van, No.8755, was hurled north of the track behind Engine No.95. On the top of its frame and at right angles to the rails rested the frame and body of Cambrian eight-wheeled composite coach, No.310, which had swept the bodywork of the light parcel van No.8755 into the wreckage of the engine.

Coach No.310, which had been added to the train at Dovey Junction, produced the least number of injuries because it was pushed sideways left off the right-hand curve by the weight of the following train. It came to rest overhanging the steep embankment down to the main road. The framework was totally removed from the bogies. However, it managed to retain its 18ft-long destination board. Passengers were able to scramble quite easily out of its compartments.

The next vehicle, Cambrian eight-wheeled 'tea-coach', No.324, was knocked off its front bogie, and the back end reared up as GWR Paddington bound eight-wheeled composite No.7730 ran into it. The whole of the inside of No.7730, including passengers, was swept into a mass of crushed wreckage at its rear end by the body of No.324.

It was from this end of the fourth express vehicle that the great majority of the deaths occurred. The number of lives lost would have been reduced by more than half if this 'running through' had not happened. The accident occurred before the general introduction of couplings that reduced sideways and vertical movement in such an event. If the carriages had stayed in line, the outcome would have been very different. It was also before the days when carriages were constructed with energy-absorbing sections that are 'sacrificed' in a crash to protect the passenger compartment.

The leading end of LNWR eight-wheeled brake coach, No.8093, was broken in, but this fifth coach was not otherwise damaged.

The 'local' engine, No.82, boiler included, had reared straight up on end over the wreck of No.95 with its tender thrown southward. The vehicle behind the engine, Cambrian eight-wheeled composite coach, No.233, was destroyed, the frame being thrown northward and the roof southward of the track. The two leading compartments of LNWR eight-wheeled third-class coach, No.260, were wrecked and the bogies knocked backward, the coach otherwise remaining intact. Luckily, there were only two passengers in the first coach of the slow train; they were the only two people on that train to be seriously injured.

Nine out of the thirteen coaches were fitted with gas lighting, but fortunately, no fire started in the wreckage, nor was any evidence found of explosion due to gas. Some passengers, however, reported breathing difficulties due to inhaling the escaping gas.

No doubt there remained in the rescuers' minds the possibility of a terrible fire breaking out as had happened at the Quintinshill accident only six years before. On that occasion, 227 soldiers of the 7th Royal Scots had died as fire broke out in a troop train that collided with a coal train – the wreckage had burnt for days.

Ironically, at Abermule a number of passengers were in greater danger of being scalded, rather than burnt. Thanks to boilers full of hot water and tenders full of cold water, any burning coals were rapidly extinguished.

A Mr Woods, who worked for Boys & Bowden of Welshpool, reported that 'a river of boiling water from the engine swept down the carriage; there was steam everywhere.'

Dr Shearer from Newtown, the first doctor at the scene of the incident.

Mr Morris' ropes and labourers being put to good use; but there is always time to pose for a photograph.

Looking back towards Newtown and Cilgwrgan. Mr Morris is first from left in the trilby.

Cambrian eight-wheeled composite No.310 – it still managed to retain its destination board!

Four sets of bogies, but they belong to the coach in front!

The combined Cambrian tea coach No.324 and GWR Paddington composite No.7730.

The breakdown train, consisting of Knapmann crane and support vehicles.

Hauling debris away to Oswestry.

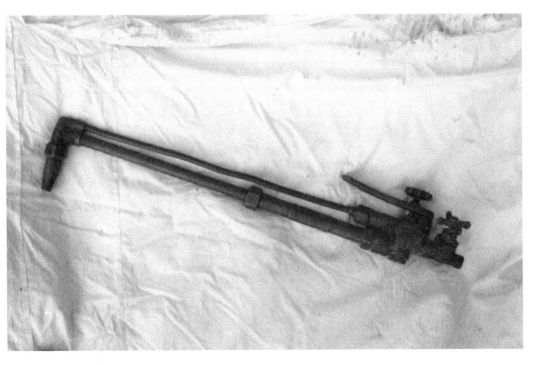

The oxyacetylene apparatus.

Above: The Abermule Triptych.

Left: Plaque made from the wood of one of the coaches involved. There are numerous examples surviving.

Below: A £1 bonus for working on the wreckage.

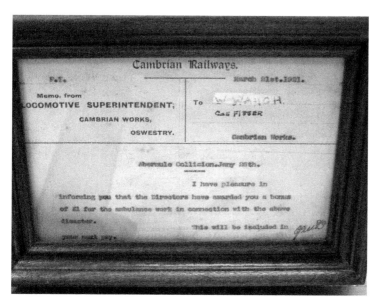

Cambrian Railways.

P.T.

March 31st.1921.

Memo. from
LOCOMOTIVE SUPERINTENDENT,
CAMBRIAN WORKS,
OSWESTRY.

To W. WAUGH.
Gas FITTER

Cambrian Works.

Abermule Collision.Jany 26th.

I have pleasure in informing you that the Directors have awarded you a bonus of £1 for the ambulance work in connection with the above disaster.

This will be included in your next pay.

The Witnesses

As the crash occurred close to the main Welshpool to Newtown road, in a well-populated area, there were a significant number of witnesses to the event, including Mr Thomas' ganger and platelayers who were working nearby. Miss Madge Parry at Cilgwrgan Farm actually saw the trains approaching each other; her mother heard the whistle and thought that their cows had strayed onto the line.

Francis Mills of Road Cottage, Llanmerewig, was at the front of the new Glanhafren smallholdings just by the crash site, and noticed the 'local' train storming up the slope, known locally as Cilgwrgan Pitch. He heard a whistle, and turning round, was just in time to witness the terrifying sight of the engines meeting: 'Scraps of metal flew through the air like shrapnel.'

George Morris, a local builder from Brynderwen Wharf, Abermule, was also working on the smallholdings. George's daughter Annie had been 'walking out' with porter Ernie Rogers for about twelve months; they later married. George's brother, Edward, was expected on the 'local' train. He was finally returning from San Francisco, he later told reporters, where he had been involved in the rebuilding of the city after the 1909 earthquake. At the scene, only baggage belonging to Edward could be found, there was no trace of him amongst the living or injured, and the family feared the worst. However, he had, for some reason not now recalled, sent his luggage on ahead and was catching the next train; the family never got over this shock.

The builders rushed across with scaffolding poles and ropes to give what help they could in rescuing the trapped passengers; unfortunately for George that was the last he saw of his building materials. One of Morris' workmen, George Maddox, broke the news to the Abermule staff when he cycled there, 'doing the journey in record time'.

Mr Pugh of Berriew Street, Welshpool, a one-time mayor of that town, was 'most upset' by the sight of blood running from the bottom of the coaches. Edna Vedmore, neé Barry, recalls that Mr Harold Williams, headmaster of the Dolforwyn Old School (all age), must have been aware that something had happened as the noise echoed around the valley. He decided to close the school and gave instructions to the older boys to go to the site to see if they could help. As the school looked over the Severn Valley towards Abermule they only had to go a few yards around the curve of the hill to see Red House Crossing, the site of the tragedy. Mr Williams immediately began to use his motorcycle to run messages around the district, there being very few telephones at that time.

One of the boys was George Hilary Smith, who was to become the last cleaner/coal loader at the Kerry engine shed prior to the line's closure to passengers in 1931.

The remainder of the younger children were directed to go straight home. Those who lived at Llanmerewig started to walk down to cross the canal bridge and the turnpike bridge over the Severn before turning right into Abermule. The usual walk was along the Mule Gorge, parallel to the Kerry branch to Fronfraith Halt, where they would turn right into Llanmerewig. Maybe one of the older children suggested that the footpath close to the railway track was followed and so the small group walked to the crash site. Edna remembers bodies laid out in the narrow pasture between the railway and the road being covered with blankets. Several men were carrying an injured or dead person on a stretcher.

The Lloyds, a well-to-do family which lived in the big house across from the crash site, Plas Trefaldwyn, were generally regarded as eccentric and that day were to prove no different. John

The local headmaster, Harold Williams, in action as a self-appointed messenger.

Maurice Edward Lloyd saw the crash and reputedly said, 'Thank God, I've no shares in the Cambrian,' before he went back inside.

Walking and running by turns, Charles Owen from the goods department at Newtown Station reached the scene of the disaster and at once joined the men who were working to remove the debris of smashed coaches to extricate the injured and dead. He himself worked with an iron bar levering the wrecked wood and metal away to reach the interior of the compartments whose partitions had splintered like crushed matchboxes:

> With the front coach thrown clear, the second one telescoped the London, sliding through it like the tray of a matchbox being shot into its cover. It crushed all the compartment partitions and passengers up against the far end, and there were no survivors. There was a guard's compartment in the Paddington coach, and the guard was a little man named Shone. I remember tying his feet together so that we could lift him out. He was dead, of course.

When fireman Owen came round, he heard, among the cries and groans, his driver's voice calling to him. Owen crawled through the wreckage and with some difficulty located his badly-injured mate who later remembered somersaulting two or three times before he came to rest underneath the third express coach. Owen wanted to fetch a doctor but Pritchard Jones did not want medical help; he only wanted to be reassured that he had been carrying the right tablet. He had examined his token before leaving Newtown and found it was correct. Could he possibly have been mistaken?

Owen, who had also been injured, began to search frantically among the twisted wreckage of the two locomotives for the tablet. He eventually managed to recover both tablets; one was their own Newtown-Abermule, but the other was for the Montgomery-Abermule section and at once the presence of the 'local' train was explained. Owen knelt beside Pritchard Jones and showed him the two tablets. 'We're all right, John; look, it was them that had the wrong tablet'. His conscience clear, Pritchard Jones consented to his fireman going off to get medical help for him; he had received a severe cut near the jugular vein in the neck, and sustained a broken collar bone and dislocated shoulder.

At the inquest, a letter was read out by the coroner from a passenger in the 'local' train who stated that he had seen: 'the young porter from Abermule, looking anxiously for the tablet' at the crash site. This was apparently about thirty minutes after the incident. Nothing further was made of this at the inquest.

William Morgan, a Cambrian traffic controller, who had been travelling on the 'local', was knocked unconscious for what he recollected to be five or six minutes. After staggering around for a while, taking in the scene of the carnage, he took both tablets off the still dazed fireman and gave them to John George, the Cambrian's chief traffic inspector, who had also been a passenger on the 'local'.

By this time inspector George had already run back to Abermule, arriving at 12.18 p.m., to organise medical assistance from Newtown and breakdown trains from Machynlleth and Oswestry – he also informed the general manager at Oswestry of the disaster. George immediately returned to the crash site on a commandeered bike, arriving back at 12.45 p.m. He then went off again to Abermule, this time with the two tablets.

Both tablets, although bearing different block names, had the number eighteen on them; this presumably referred to the station number for Abermule. The 'deadly tablet' now became an instrument of mercy. In the presence of witnesses, at 1.08 p.m., Inspector George placed it in the Abermule-Montgomery machine, lettered side downwards. This action cleared that section and allowed the breakdown train from Oswestry, headed by 0-6-0 Jones goods engine, No.31, to proceed to the crash.

Signalman Humphreys at Montgomery should have received that 'train out of section' advice from Abermule at about 12.01 p.m. – just around the time that Lewis and Thompson finally looked at their instruments. The other tablet, the 'Newtown-Abermule' was immediately locked away – no doubt it had been used to free the Newtown instrument to allow help to come from that direction. The 'deadly tablet' was later released by the telegraphic technician and locked away by Mr Sellars of the General Manager's office. Presumably, from then on the system was operated with the mandatory presence of a pilotman on the footplate of any engine which moved. This supplanted the tablet system for the duration of the restoration of track and service. There are local memories of Moat Lane guards undertaking this task on both sides of the accident; Arthur Davies, who rescued the tea ladies, was later pressed into service for this duty, being on the staff at Newtown.

Help arrived from the south by rail within an hour. It came from Llanidloes where there happened to be an engine 'in steam'. Various wagons were loaded up with anything which might be useful and the train called at Moat Lane and Newtown to pick up as many men as possible. The breakdown train from Oswestry, consisting of a Knapmann crane and five assorted coaches, arrived at 1.30 p.m. Before dark, an engine on the other side of the wreckage was attached to the undamaged portion of the 'down' train and moved it away towards Abermule. The reared-up express engine fell back to earth with a tremendous crash as its support was removed. Portions of the engines, steel coach-frames, etc., were found to be so entangled and in such a perilous position, 'that oxy-acetylene plant was utilised for cutting up the steelwork into weights that

Sergeant Woodfine tries to keep some semblance of order.

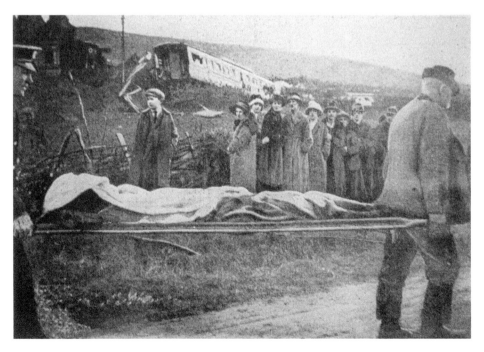

On their way to the infirmary at Newtown.

could be handled by the mobile steam crane.' This would cause no comment nowadays, but at the time, there were only two oxyacetylene sets in the whole of Montgomeryshire. The one available to the rescuers was owned by the obviously progressive company of J. Peter Jones & Sons: Steam Transport and Rolling Contractor.

The wreckage was so inextricably locked together that it took the breakdown gangs under George Macdonald, the chief engineer of the Cambrian, over fifty hours of continuous work to clear the line.

Staff from the Cambrian bridge department at Caersws worked with the Oswestry and Machynlleth crane crews as recovery proceeded over extended shifts – there was a mess coach and a sleeping coach on the 'down' side of the site in the charge of Joseph Smith Jones, who was on light duties because of gas injuries during the war. The paraffin floodlights normally used for bridge inspections were brought from Caersws; this enabled the work to continue throughout the night. Railway employees engaged in the work were awarded bonuses of £1 for their salvage work; this was paid to them in their following wage packet.

The Dead and Injured

Local people from Abermule, Aberbecan, and Llanmerewig brought along bed sheets for bandages and gallons of hot drinks to revive the spirits of those involved. The first doctors arrived on the scene about thirty minutes after the accident – the subsequent rescue operation was well organised by Deputy Chief Constable Williams and Sergeant Davies of Newtown Police Station.

The policeman prominent in many photographs of the incident was Sergeant Woodfine who lived locally. By strange chance, all the constables of the Montgomeryshire Police Force were assembled at Newtown for their first-ever examination and they were rushed to the scene of the disaster. They arrived at approximately 1.30 p.m. and remained there until 2.00 a.m. the following morning; they maintained a reduced presence until the line was cleared. The Cambrian Railways also had its own police force – about fifty officers – but there is no record of their attendance.

Not only on the day of the disaster, but right up until the track was reopened, several hundred sightseers visited the scene and watched the task of clearing the debris. A local paper reported: 'The police had struggled to maintain good order against a crowd which wanted to see anything and everything.' There was a report that the young factory girls at Pryce Jones' factory in Newtown wanted to go en bloc to the site to enquire about relatives and friends, but the management locked them in.

Fleets of vehicles were soon transporting the injured to the Montgomeryshire Infirmary at Newtown – included in these was the motor ambulance driven by Harold Bennett Lloyd. Whilst Dr Shearer of Newtown was in attendance at the crash, Dr Clark directed the medical and surgical services at the infirmary. Other doctors involved were: Davies-Rheese of Caersws; Davies of Llanidloes; Williams of Machynlleth; Cartwright, Marshall and Stevenson of Oswestry; Crump, Fowell, Higgins and Thomas of Welshpool.

Arrangements for the reception of the victims at the infirmary were made with 'commendable promptitude' and everything that was possible was done by Dr Bellamy and Dr R. Owen Morris who received the cases. The matron and the regular nursing staff were supplemented by Nurse Mary Bebb of Newtown, Nurse Evans of Llandinam, Nurse Williams of Llanfyllin, Nurse Vaughan-Owen of Llanidloes and Nurse Hughes of Sarn. The matron, Miss E. Lumley, and her staff were thoroughly praised for their work over the next few days, as was the secretary of the infirmary, Mr E.C. Morgan.

Within three-quarters of an hour, the St John's Ambulance Brigade detachment under First Officer Morris and Sergeant Jones, set off from Welshpool by special train. They were accompanied by Dr Cartwright, Dr Marshall and Dr Stevenson. By the time that they arrived, only one man, Lewis Brookes, remained trapped. All casualties were removed from the scene by late afternoon; the remaining, uninjured, passengers were taken to Welshpool by car.

The Earl and Countess of Powys visited the infirmary that evening and on the following day they sent a 'consignment of dainties and choice fruit'. The Cambrian chairman, David Davies, in turn, sent 'large quantities of poultry, fruit and invalid dishes of the most suitable kind.'

The King and Queen sent a message of sympathy via Major Davies:

> The King and Queen are much concerned to hear of the terrible railway accident involving great loss of life. Their Majesties deeply sympathise with the relatives of those who have been killed and hope that the injured are making good progress.
> Signed. Private Secretary, Sandringham.

The following reply was sent by the chairman:

> I beg to thank your Majesties for your kind message of sympathy which I have conveyed to the relatives of the victims of this terrible disaster and to the injured in hospital. Your Majesties will be pleased to know that everything possible is being done to succour the injured at Montgomery County Infirmary, Newtown. With two exceptions, all are making good progress.

The Prince of Wales sent his personal message of condolence, as did the National Union of Railwaymen.

Eleven passengers and three Cambrian operating staff were killed on the spot; twenty seriously-injured people were taken to hospital, and three of these died later.

The eleven passengers killed outright at Red House Crossing were:

Nurse Margaret Ella Gethin (24), Boot Stores, Llandinam	(E)
Mrs Ethel Lewis Harper (35), 3 Albany Road, Harbourne, Birmingham	(E)
Victor Leslie Harper (19), (not related to Ethel) 8 Gas Street, Newtown	(E)
James Henderson (53), Garden City, Machynlleth	(E)
John Jones (61), Hafod-Awelon, Aberystwyth	(E)
Ralph Denzil Onslow (17), Mount Severn, Llanidloes	(E)
Guildford Dennis Onslow (16), Mount Severn, Llanidloes	(E)
Captain Harold Owen Owen (24), Garthgwynion, Machynlleth	(E)
Miss Gwendolyn Priscilla Scott Owen (31), Cefngwifed, Tregynon	(E)
Miss C. Evelyn Pryse-Rice (24), Llwynybrain, Landovery	(E)
Alfred Trethewey (28), 13 Gold Hawk Road, Shepherd's Bush, London	(E)

The three deceased railwaymen were:

Albert W. (Bertie) Evans (25), Fireman, 12 Mount Street, Llanidloes	(L)
George Jones (68), Driver, 9 Hafren Terrace, Llanidloes	(L)
Edward Shone (69) Guard, 4 Stanley Street, Aberystwyth	(E)

One of Shone's sons was a signalman at Aberystwyth and he had signalled his father off that morning – as was their custom, they waved as the train passed the box; he was later to identify his father's body at Newtown. Shone had seven sons – two others were driver and guard on the Cambrian. A special train brought colleagues to his funeral from different parts of the system. It was held on a Sunday so that as many as possible could attend. The procession was lead by the mayor of Aberystwyth – also present were a very large number of other civic and church dignitaries. The funeral was held at Holy Trinity Church where Edward had been a sidesman and a member of the P.C.C. He had been a leading light in both the local Co-operative Society and the local branch of the NUR. Not only did

Above: Aberystwyth signal box where father and son waved to each other on that fateful morning.

Rightt: Guard Edward Shone; 'one of the cheeriest men in the company's service'

two of the deceased railwaymen come from Llanidloes, but, of the five passengers who got on there intending to travel further than Newtown, three were killed and one was injured.

Three people died later of their injuries at the Infirmary:

George L. Slade (43), Westley Street, Manchester	(E)
Lord Herbert Vane-Tempest (58), Plas, Machynlleth – on that day	(E)
Leversedge (Lewis) Brookes (21), 8 Severn Villas, Llanidloes – on 1 February	(E)

The three railwaymen injured were:

Edwin Chetwood, Albert Road, Oswestry, Guard (head wound)	(L)
John Pritchard Jones, Trinity Road, Aberystwyth, Driver, (severed neck artery)	(E)
John Owen, Fireman (leg injury)	(E)

The passengers injured, including two off-duty company employees, travelling 'on the cushions' (★) were:

R.E. Beckitt, Quarry House, Shrewsbury (minor cuts and bruises)
Samuel Beddowes, Holbach Road, Oswestry (face and back)
Richard Ernest Davies, Fordestyn, Wrexham (head and foot)
William Davies, Beeches, Berriew (Cambrian Foreman, Welshpool)
James Sydney Edwards ★, 7 Vine Cottages, Oswestry (Fireman) (wrist and leg)
S. Humphreys ★, Caersws, (Driver) (scalded)
Ernest Clifford Harper, Surveyor's Dept., G.P.O., Shrewsbury (minor bruises)
J.R. Owen, Maesgwyn Road, Wrexham (head and arm)
John Rudge, White Grit, Minsterley (head and face)
James Dugald Shaw, Nantoes, Aberystwyth (broken arm and leg)
Miss Annie Tomkins (leg and hand) and her sister (both Cambrian Tea Car attendants)
Miss Barbara Tomkins (bruises to head and leg), Derwen House, Preesgweene
Christopher Walton, (head and back) London House, Aberystwyth, and his son, Kenneth (head and knee)

Driver Jones and Fireman Evans of the slow train were burnt to death in the wreckage of their engine. Their injuries were appalling as they had been trapped in the burning coals ejected from the firebox; the newspaper accounts ghoulishly reported that their heads had actually been burnt off. It also gives further unnecessary details of their extensive injuries. They had obviously made no attempt to get off the engine.

The guard of the express train, Edward Shone, was killed by massive injuries caused by splintered woodwork in the express Paddington coach. He was a red-bearded little man, said to be 'probably one of the company's cheeriest servants.' Guard Shone had charge of the train as far as Welshpool where it was divided, and he then continued with the Shrewsbury-Paddington portion.

Guard Thomas who had joined the train at Moat Lane Junction would have continued on with the Manchester section as far as Whitchurch. Thomas was riding in the guard's van at the rear of the train, sitting in the boxed-in guard's seat with its padded sides. This stopped him being thrown across the van when the impact occurred.

Lord Herbert Vane-Tempest was a director of the Cambrian Railways Co. As a railway company, it is never good policy to involve one of the directors in an accident, but to do it twice to the same family!

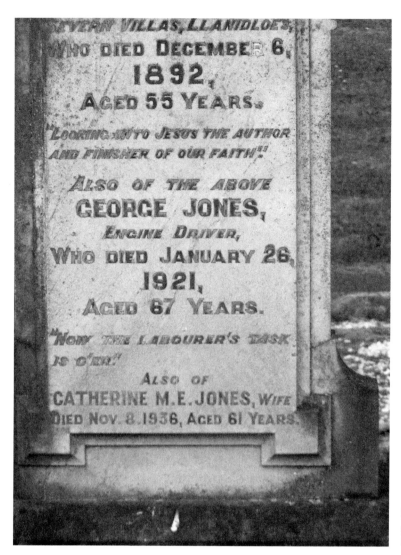

VERN VILLAS, LLANIDLOES,
WHO DIED DECEMBER 6,
1892,
AGED 55 YEARS.

"LOOKING INTO JESUS THE AUTHOR
AND FINISHER OF OUR FAITH".

ALSO OF THE ABOVE
GEORGE JONES,
ENGINE DRIVER,
WHO DIED JANUARY 26,
1921,
AGED 67 YEARS.

"NOW THE LABOURER'S TASK
IS O'ER."

ALSO OF
CATHERINE M.E. JONES, WIFE
DIED NOV. 8 1936, AGED 61 YEARS.

Driver Jones'
grave at Dolhafren
Cemetery, Llanidloes.

On the evening of 8 November 1869, a 'down' passenger train collided with a heavy double-headed goods train which was shunting at Carno, causing two of the carriages at the rear of the passenger train to break away and run unhindered for 5 miles back down the incline. On the train was Lord Herbert's father, the Earl Vane-Tempest. Somehow the coaches managed to keep to the rails as they rattled at ever-increasing speed through Pontdolgoch and Caersws before finally coming to a rest just before the level-crossing on the Llanidloes road. The solitary occupant of the second coach, a commercial traveller from Manchester, walked the mile or so with the Earl to Moat Lane Junction where a doctor was summoned to attend to the Earl's head wound.

Fifty-two years later, Lord Herbert Vane-Tempest died of a head wound at Abermule.

Dr Alfred Shearer, who attended to Lord Herbert, was a native of Orkney, and qualified at Edinburgh University in 1896. He entered general practice at Newtown in 1900. Originally he had 'done his rounds' on horseback, but he became a pioneer motorist prior to the First

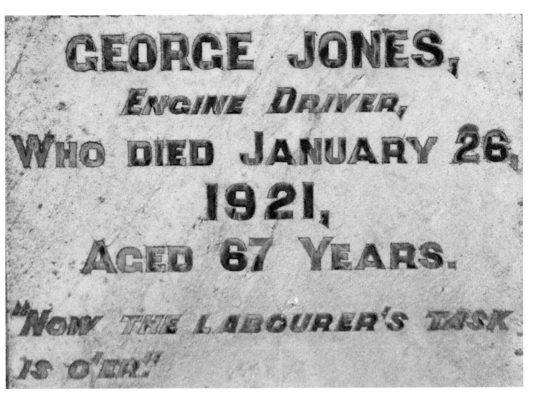

'Now the labourer's task is o'er.'

World War with his first vehicle, EP14, possibly one of the ubiquitous Austin 7s. When Doctor Shearer arrived just after 12.30 p.m., he was sent directly to Lord Herbert who was taken to the infirmary as soon as he was freed from the wreckage; he died in hospital about 4.30 p.m.

His Lordship had been on his way to his home in London, Londonderry House in Park Lane, to shortly join his friend Lord Derby on a visit to the Riviera. Aged fifty-eight, he was the third son of the fifth Marquess of Londonderry; a favourite with royalty, he had on several memorable occasions entertained the King and Queen and other members of the Royal Family at the Plas, Machynlleth (now Celtica). He was a former lord-in-waiting to His Majesty; he was also a JP, chairman of the Urban Council, and Master of Hounds; his clubs in London were the Turf and the Bachelors. His death caused the Garron Tower Estate in Co. Antrim, Ireland, to pass into the possession of Winston Churchill, Secretary of State for War, who was his first cousin once removed.

The Waltons, father and son, had started their journey at Aberystwyth and were going to Malvern where Mr Walton's mother was seriously ill. Christopher Walton had been standing in the corridor of the Paddington coach when the collision occurred and though he was bleeding badly, he had managed to scramble out through a window to get help for his trapped son. Young Kenneth, about seven years of age, was the first to be rescued; though not badly hurt he was too dazed to speak.

The rescuers moved them both to the top of a bank where they were attended to by a nurse, Miss Elwell, from Dolgelly. This lady had been a passenger, and though badly shaken herself, did splendid work attending to the injured.

The first of the rescuers into action was William Henry Davies, a foreman with the Cambrian at Welshpool station, who had been a passenger on the express. Bill was thrown clear with such force that from then on he was known as 'Davies the rocket.' He was apparently a relative of George Morris, the builder mentioned earlier. Davies ran back to the remains of the Paddington coach and saw Leversedge Brookes and Lord Vane-Tempest trapped inside, but was unable to reach them. Then he, Guard Ewart Thomas and the Abermule track maintenance gang —who had been working nearby — made a hole in the roof and rescued young Kenneth Walton. It was the ganger of those men who had been arranging for the wood transport with sub-inspector Thomas about two hours earlier.

Davies had been the guard on one of the Cambrian goods trains that had crashed head-on at Park Hall on 18 January 1918. On that occasion he had been thrown out of his brake van onto the track; he had never fully recovered from his injuries.

If Ewart Thomas, assistant guard on the express, had not stopped to talk with Davies on this occasion, then he too would have been killed along with Edward Shone. Shone had passed down the corridor to the brake compartment in the Paddington carriage to sort luggage just two minutes before the crash. Just over ten years later, Thomas was the guard on the last service to run on the Kerry branch on 7 February 1931. He had been born in the Van Lead Mines cottages around 1890.

A local preacher was seen with his coat off and smashing away with an axe to get to those trapped inside the wreckage. Five of the coaches carried fire extinguishers, salvage equipment and first-aid boxes; these totalled four ladders, nine crowbars, nine axes, six saws and four hammers.

Four disabled soldiers from Welshpool, William Harris, Thomas Jones, Harry Evans and Alf Aymes, who went to the Newtown Infirmary every day for treatment, helped in the rescue after escaping uninjured from the 'local' train. One of them gave first aid to the express driver.

Opposite: Guard Ewart Thomas, on the left, taking a break from shunting the Kerry goods at Newtown, with Vic Corfield.

Right: Mrs Ethel Harper; her husband survived because he wanted a newspaper.

Quite early on in the rescue proceedings, a woman was brought out dead; her features were unrecognizable. On her wrist was a handbag, which on opening was found to contain a small box with a gold brooch inside. A man at once cried out in agony: 'Oh God! It's my Polly.'

Herbert Harper of Hazelwell, Birmingham, later identified the body of his sister-in-law Ethel, the wife of Mr Ernest Clifford Harper, a Post Office surveyor. Ernest was too ill to give evidence at the inquest, being laid up at Newton Hall. His occupation had necessitated a lot of travelling, and on the previous day he and his wife had travelled from Machynlleth to Shrewsbury. Mrs Harper was thirty-five and the couple lived at 13 Albany Road, Harbourne, Birmingham.

Some had
Lucky Escapes

Although he had lost his wife, Ernest Harper had a lucky escape himself. He had got off at Newtown to buy a newspaper at the W.H. Smith's bookstall, but the train began to move off so jumped into a coach near the rear of the express just before it departed.

George Bell, a commercial traveller from Greenwich, had been thrown out into the field from a smashed toilet compartment in the leading coach of the express. According to Bryan Kinsey of Penyffordd, Abermule, who was on the road virtually under the crash site when it happened, 'he went bowling down the field like a rabbit shot in the forelegs'. George was unhurt, but dazed and somewhat embarrassed when rescuers found him.

The assistant secretary to the Cambrian general manager, Mr T. C. Sellers, had been travelling on the 'local' train on company business. He had seated himself in the first carriage at Oswestry, but something made him get out and go the rear carriage.

The Tomkins sisters worked together in the Cambrian tea car, which ran between Aberystwyth and Shrewsbury; they had served his Lordship with a cup of tea shortly beforehand, 'price 3d, freshly brewed'. Arthur Richard Davies managed to smash his way in with an axe and rescue them. The sisters had also been involved in the Talerddig cutting accident eight days before, when the same passenger service ran into a landslide. Two engines had been derailed and the first engine, No.54, turned onto its side. No carriages left the line and no one was injured. It was not unusual for Cambrian employees, trains or equipment to be involved in more than one accident. The sisters had been remarkable lucky on both occasions.

Miss Gwen Morgan of Mornington Villa, Bradford, had been staying with her uncle and aunt, Mr and Mrs Edward Morgan, at Plas-cae-crwn, Newtown. She escaped unhurt from the crash due to the fact that as she was just about to step into the London coach at Newtown an obliging porter informed her that she would be able to travel further without changing if she took a seat in the Manchester coach. Her luggage, including her golf clubs, was transferred so: 'by that means my life was for a certainty saved'.

One of the most thankful persons stood at the scene of the accident was Mr Morrow, a commercial traveller from Wallasey. 'I was doing business with a tradesman in Newtown but discovered I just had bare time to catch the 11.24; with apologies to my customer I broke off business and made a rush for the station. As a rule I ride in the through [Paddington] coach but upon getting on to the platform I had no time for choice and promptly jumped into a rear carriage.'

Mr James of Shrewsbury, a well-known newspaper agent, said that at Welshpool something caused him to change his compartment, and he went more to the rear of the train. Although the compartment into which he changed was partially telescoped, and he was badly shaken, he otherwise escaped injury. The compartment in which he had first seated himself was smashed to splinters.

Mr Alban S. James of Fern Villa, Underdale Road, Shrewsbury, was on the 'local' train, and had changed from the first coach to the second one at Welshpool – he never knew why. Mr John Williams, chief audit inspector from Head Office, played a heroic part in the rescue work; that he escaped serious injury was probably due to the fact that he was riding in a heavily padded first-class compartment in the front portion of the slow train.

'A cup of tea, m'Lord?' A piece of crockery that survived the accident, and was turned into a piece of memorabilia.

James Dugald Shaw, a young South American, was travelling from Aberystwyth back to Harrow School. His father, Alexander, was in South America and his mother was resident in France at that time. The young chap stayed with the distantly-related Powell family at Nantoes Hall in the Paith Valley, near Aberystwyth, during his school holidays. He was in the Paddington carriage in a compartment on his own, in front of Lord Vane-Tempest's, and heard him call out for help, but could not assist as he himself was injured. After being imprisoned for half an hour, James was rescued, though his left arm and left leg were broken. On returning to Nantoes, he moved from his two-room apartment upstairs to similar accommodation on the ground floor until his injuries were healed. He soon returned to his passion for owning racehorses.

Mr A.E. Beckitt of Quarry View, Shrewsbury, a representative of Fairle & Co., sugar refiners of Liverpool, said:

> I was in the front coach having a conversation with two of my friends, Mr J. Owen of Wrexham, and Mr Samuel Beddowes of Oswestry representing Messrs Masefield, Jam Manufacturers of Liverpool, both of whom are now in hospital. I went off to sleep.

Mr Beddowes recalled that:

> When I regained my senses I found myself smoking a pipe. It appears that someone took the pipe out of my pocket, lit it, and placed it in my mouth with a purpose of assisting me back to consciousness. Having to walk on sticks in consequence of rheumatism it was impossible for

CAMBRIAN RAILWAYS.
FIRST-CLASS TARIFF.

Tea . . (Freshly Made) per cup 3d.		Whisky . . per glass 3d. & 4d.	
Pot of Tea, with Bread and Butter, per person 6d.		Brandy . . „ 4d. & 6d.	
Coffee . . . per cup 3d.		Rum, Gin or Hollands „ 3d.	
Cocoa or Chocolate . „ 3d.		Claret . . . . „ 3d.	
Sandwiches . . . each 2d.		Port or Sherry . . „ 4d.	
Pastry and Cakes (Various) . „ 1d.		Bitters . . . . „ 3d. & 4d.	
Pies . . . . . „ 6d.		Vermouth . . . . „ . 4d.	
Chocolates and Sweets (Various) 1d., 3d., 6d. & 1s.		Curacao, Kummel, Menthe or Benedictine . . per glass 6d.	
Milk (see Notices) . per glass 2d.		Ginger or Cherry Brandy . „ 4d.	
"Oxo" Fluid Beef . per cup 4d.		Cherry Whisky . . „ 4d.	
Apollinaris . . per ½-bottle 6d.		Sloe Gin . . . „ 4d.	
„ (Splits) . . . 4d.		Ale or Stout . . „ 2½d.	
Perrier (Splits) . . . 4d.		„ „ . per bottle 3½d.	
Soda, Seltzer or Lemonade , small 2d.		Lager Beer . . „ 3½d.	
Ginger Ale, Dry (Splits) . . 3d.		Cider . . . „ 4d.	
Ginger Beer . . . . 2d.		Cigars . each 2d., 3d., 4d. & 6d.	
Ginger Wine . . per glass 2d.		Cigarettes . . . . each 1d.	
Lime Juice . . „ 2d.		„ per pkt 1d., 3d., 6d. & 9d.	
		Tobacco 1-oz . 4½d., 5d., 5½d. & 6d.	

Wines (See Special List.)

☛ SPECIAL NOTICE.
SPIERS & POND SUPPLY
LUNCHEON & TEA BASKETS
to all the following Railways, viz.:—
LONDON & SOUTH WESTERN, SOUTH EASTERN & CAMBRIAN.

1518 — CAMBRIAN RAILWAY. August, 1915.   Spiers & Pond Limited, Refreshment Contractors.   Central Offices: 35, New Bridge Street, E.6.

The refreshments that were available from the line's catering contractors, Spiers & Pond.

Master James Shaw, also on his way back to Harrow School after the Christmas holidays.

me to get out of the carriage myself, but thanks to the assistance of two persons I was removed and placed upon the embankment.

A number of other passengers had similar narrow escapes – others, however, were not so lucky.

Captain Harold Owen Owen had survived five years with the 6th Battalion Royal Welch Fusiliers in France and Mesopotamia, returning home in 1919. He had attended Harrow School between September 1909 and late 1913. He was a keen sportsman and a member of the OTC. By 1910 he was the senior male member of the family and became a director of the well-known Liverpool firm, Messrs Owen Owen Ltd.

At the time of his death, Harold was involved in negotiations to build a new road across the valley at Garthgwynion, near Machynlleth, one of the family homes. It was the signing of these documents on 25 January that delayed his return to London by a day. Family tradition maintains that Harold was invited into the compartment of Lord Herbert Vane-Tempest to share the journey with him.

His body was cremated at Liverpool and his ashes buried in the family vault at Machynlleth Nonconformist Cemetery. The burial service was held on 29 January and conducted by the Bishop of Bangor – his ashes were carried to the cemetery on a gun carriage, the casket being draped with a Union Jack. The family kept a guest book at Garthgwynion, to record the comings and goings of the family and guests. The entry for 26 January 1921 reads 'Harold – asleep.' He was twenty-five years old. He left £200 in his will to Harrow School for 'athletic purposes'.

James Henderson had been Lord Vane-Tempest's valet for twenty-four years, and was buried in a grave next to his master in St Peter's churchyard at Machynlleth; their bodies were conveyed to the church in the same procession and they were interred in identical coffins. Henderson lived at Garden City, Machynlleth. The *Montgomery Express* was sufficiently crass as to report that his wife had come into £1,000 under *The Daily Mail* accident scheme as she was registered as a regular reader of that paper.

Captain Harold Owen Owen.

Later in the year, on 18 December, the Bishop of Bangor dedicated a stained glass window at Machynlleth parish church in memory of Lord Vane-Tempest.

The Onslow brothers, Guildford Denzil (aged sixteen) and Ralph Denis (aged seventeen), from Llanidloes were also on their way back to school at Harrow. They were in the upper fifth and the lower sixth, and lodged in Sir Arthur Hort's House, Newlands. Their father, Colonel Arthur Loftus Onslow, who was a Llanidloes magistrate and managing director of the Van and Nantiago mines, had told them to get into the GWR's London carriage at Newtown. As the youngest, Guildford, was being lifted from the wreckage, an orange rolled from his pocket onto the line. He was the first of those killed to be removed.

The bodies of the Onslow boys were conveyed by the Red Cross motor ambulance from Newtown on the Friday evening and placed in Llanidloes parish church where a short service was conducted by Canon E.O. Jones in the presence of the immediate family. On Saturday, after

James Henderson's grave alongside his master's at Machynlleth Cemetery.

a brief service in the church the bodies were conveyed in the ambulance to Dolhafren Cemetery – no further interments were being made in the churchyard.

The boys are buried in a joint grave, now sadly in poor condition. Dolhafren Cemetery is divided in two sections by the chapels; traditionally the lower section was reserved for 'ordinary people' whilst the ground nearer the road was the resting place of the upper classes such as the Onslows. Mrs Onslow broke this convention when she insisted that in death her two boys were the same as everyone else, and she had them buried among the ordinary graves. Colonel and Mrs Onslow used to visit the local primary school to talk to the children about foreign lands.

On 29 June at the 350th Anniversary Speech Day at Harrow School, the two Onslow boys and Harold Owen Owen were commemorated.

The father of Nurse Gethin, who was in her second year of training to be a midwife at the London Temperance Hospital, had a terrible ordeal in watching the removal of a

Lord Vane-Tempest's grave.

Lord Herbert Vane-Tempest.

young woman's body from the wreckage. He had seen his daughter off at Llandinam and remembered that the last thing he saw of her alive was the white cuff of her uniform sleeve as she waved him goodbye; it was also the first thing he saw at the crash site, sticking out of the wreckage. Yet, such was the terrible nature of the her injuries, face and hair being covered and matted with blood, that Mr Gethin was still uncertain as to whether the dead body was that of his daughter. A search in the girl's pockets by a railwayman proved however that his fears were only too true.

It took five hours to free Leversedge (Lewis) Brookes. He had been in the GWR Paddington coach of the express and was severely crushed from the pelvis down. Just as darkness began to descend on the rescue operations the tangle of wreckage that had been GWR coach No.7730 at length yielded to saw, hammer, ropes, and brute force. While Doctor Shearer stood above Brookes shielding his body, the corpses were reverently drawn out and carried off on stretchers: 'Following which the crowd gave way to its feelings of pent up joy as Brookes was lifted by many strong arms and placed onto a stretcher. He was immediately motored to the infirmary.'

Brookes died on 1 February in the infirmary; he had nearly died on the Wednesday night and again on the Thursday morning, but after that he had begun to rally and his condition continued to improve up to Saturday when he died through shock.

Lewis was buried in Dolhafren Cemetery; unfortunately there is now no headstone on the badly tended grave. He had seen active service since 1917 in France, Italy and Russia and was wounded three times, including being bayoneted within a week of reaching the front lines. He was the only survivor of a unit of six signallers in one engagement. On the day in question, he was returning from sick leave at his parents' home in Llanidloes to Wolverhampton Hospital where he was being treated for 'poisoning of the stomach' as a result of being gassed. He had been the goalkeeper for Llanidloes Football Club the previous year, but at the time in question, played for Bilston Football Club as he worked at Wolverhampton Post Office.

Miss Gwendolyn (Dolly) Scott Owen, whose body was the last to be removed from the crash, had come home for her father's funeral a week or so beforehand. William Scott Owen was the estate agent for the Gregynog Estate; he lived at Cefngwifed Mansion and was a keen local historian. The restoration of the church occurred around 1893 under his guidance. By this time, the estate was owned by Misses Gwendolyn and Margaret Davies, who later gifted the estate to Aberystwyth University. Dolly was a talented linguist and artist, and excelled at country pursuits; she spent most of her time in London.

Dolly's sister, Marjory, a Red Cross nurse stationed in Mesopotamia, whom she had not seen for many years, had missed their father's funeral and only arrived back the day before the disaster,

G. Dennis Onslow (16) was in the Upper Fifth at Harrow. Ralph D. Onslow (17) was in the Sixth Form at Harrow. The two Harrow boys who were killed were on their way back to school. Their father was waiting to meet them at Paddington.

Dennis and Ralph Onslow.

The Onslow boys' joint grave at Dolhafren Cemetery, Llanidloes.

virtually just in time to see her sister off. She later had the unpleasant task of identifying her sister's body. Dolly and her father are interred in matching memorials in Gregynog churchyard.

The body of Victor Lesley Harper of 8 The Bank, Newtown, was identified by his brother, Ernest Harper, a wool sorter. Victor was a postal employee at Welshpool and that week was working late hours. He came from Welshpool on the Wednesday morning with the 9.05 a.m. train and left again for Welshpool on the express to return to work. He was nineteen years of age and was in lodgings at 36 Salop Road, Welshpool. He began his Post Office career in Newtown during November 1914, and:

> By his own zeal succeeded in passing the necessary educational examination and eventually became employed as a sorting clerk and telegraphist in the Shrewsbury Post Office in June 1920. Hearing of a vacancy in the Welshpool office in August of the same year he successfully applied for a transfer in order to be near his home at Newtown. He was of a cheerful disposition and possessed a deep bass voice; he could be frequently heard in the office humming popular tunes.

The chapels dividing Dolhafren Cemetery.

Although only in his teens, he was a hard-working and conscientious member and officer of the Newtown Baptist church where he: 'took exceptional interest in the work and only under extraordinary circumstances was he ever absent from their meetings'.

Mr Cyril Thomas Davies, 8 Stanley Road, Aberystwyth, a pianoforte agent, had identified the body of Mr Alfred Trethewey 13 Gold Hawk Road, London. Cyril was a friend of the deceased who was a respected pianoforte maker and instructor; Alfred was a married man with no children. Mr Trethewey had arrived in Aberystwyth on Monday and stayed at Mr Davies' house until the Wednesday morning for a short break from work. His wife sent him a telegram saying that he should have a good rest and not rush back home. However, he was keen to return to work and wired back: 'Coming home today. Arrive Paddington 5.25.' He got into the through coach for Paddington.

Mr G.L. Slade represented the firm of Messrs Thomas Collier & Co. of Manchester, and travelled in umbrellas and gloves. He lived at Harboro Street, Chorlton-on-Medlock, Manchester; his body was identified by Mr Albert Sumpers of Vicarage Road, Chester, a senior traveller for the same firm. Mr Slade was well known to tradesmen in local towns and left a wife and two children. The last firm he called upon was Messrs Evans & Parry's Drapery at Llanidloes; he left the shop with only a small margin of time to catch the 11.20 a.m. train. He was going to Welshpool, breaking his journey there, before proceeding back to Manchester. 'He was a popular and trustworthy traveller'.

Nurse Ella Gethin, student nurse returning to London.

Mr John Jones of Hafod-Awelon, Aberystwyth, was going to see his daughter in London. He was sixty-two years of age and a retired, successful businessman from London. About three years previously he had purchased property in the vicinity of Aberystwyth, where he had built a fine house for himself and his family. He left a widow, a son, John Hellos Jones, and two daughters. Mr Jones senior was a member of Shiloh C.M. Chapel and at the time was filling the post of senior superintendent of the Sunday School.

For some unknown reason, Miss Gwendolyn Evelyn Nesta Pryce-Rice was never mentioned in any of the obituaries, though hers was a well-known family in the Aberystwyth area. Apparently her body was unmarked, and it was speculated that she might have been suffocated. It is believed that she was returning to Market Harborough.

Fireman Bert William Evans was the second son of Mr and Mrs Penry Evans of 12 Mount Street, Llanidloes. Whilst he was at the front in early 1917, his wife had died in childbirth; he arrived back home a day late for the joint funeral. During the attack on Pomperian Ridge he was severely gassed – so badly affected was he that he was left on the ground for dead and when his comrades went to him again he had been stripped of all his personal equipment including pocket watch, wallet, money, etc. Even though he returned to work on the Cambrian, it can be assumed that he never really overcame that series of events.

His funeral took place at St Clements church burial ground, Rhayader on Saturday afternoon; his remains being laid to rest beside those of his late wife and child. The coffin was brought by

rail arriving about 2.00 p.m. when 'a vast assemblage' gathered at the station. All businesses and private houses were closed and blinds drawn. The coffin was draped with the Union Jack as a token of his war service.

All those killed were placed in a temporary morgue in the cloakroom and ladies' waiting room at Newtown Station and guarded by police officers. Nurse Lathom had the unpleasant duty of dealing with the badly mutilated bodies, whilst railway clerk John Morris helped with the detailing of personal property and effects. Six of the deceased were removed from there on the Thursday afternoon after the inquest – the rest were moved on the Friday. The paper noted that '…many people assembled at the station and watched with mournful interest the removal of the victims.' Many of the funerals took place on the Saturday.

The Cambrian meanwhile had laid on fleets of charabancs and luggage vehicles to overcome the problem of the disrupted service. Long-distance freight and passenger trains would have been diverted via Ruabon and Dolgellau to the coast and at Builth Road for Shrewsbury on other companies' lines. Apparently this was all so well organised that journey times were hardly affected. Adding to the confusion and traffic was the sudden influx of the members of the press from all over the country who also took up virtually all the hotel accommodation.

The line was checked when an engine ran the route from Abermule to Newtown shortly after midday on the Saturday. This was following Colonel Pringle's fact-finding trip from Oswestry to Abermule for the official inquiry. The 2.30 a.m. from Newtown to Oswestry officially reopened the service – this was a day ahead of the estimated time. However, the wreckage remained piled high on either side of the track for a long time to come; a grim reminder of the event for nervous travellers.

Opposite: Memorials to Gwendolyn and William Scott Owen at Tregynon Church.

Right: Alfred Trethewey; his wife had told him not to rush back from his short break away at the seaside.

Below: The wreckage was to remain for quite a while before the site was finally cleared.

Sid Lloyd, nephew of the express driver involved in the accident, was possibly the last person to drive a steam engine over that stretch of line, and recalled that it was: 'always a strange feeling driving an express from Newtown to Abermule.'

It was proposed locally to erect a memorial stone at the site of the crash; one suggestion was that it could be a 'large undressed block of limestone from Pant Quarry, about 10 tons or so in weight, with a brass inscription plate let into it. This stone weathers well and keeps its colour.' The Cambrian initially agreed to this, but later gave 200 guineas (£210) to the funds of the Montgomeryshire Infirmary at Newtown instead – this was 'in grateful recognition of the services rendered by that institution'.

The Inquest

The coroner's inquest was opened in the Police Court, Newtown, at noon on Thursday 27 January, with Mr J.T.C. Gittings presiding. The first proceedings were to hear evidence of the identity of those killed in the crash; during this process, the jury visited the makeshift morgue. After this harrowing exercise was completed, the coroner released the bodies to the relatives, and adjourned the proceedings until the following Wednesday.

The coroner had asked the Board of Trade for an inspector to help conduct the inquest. When the proceedings reopened, that technical assistance, and the 'examination in chief' for his own inquiry, was carried out by Colonel Pringle, chief officer of the Railway Inspectorate who sat alongside the coroner.

The Railway Inspectorate had been set up through the Regulation of Railways Acts, passed in 1840, to investigate the ever-increasing number of incidents. Colonel Pringle was one of that body's more famous inspectors, all of whom were drawn from the ranks of the Royal Engineers. He had carried out the enquiry at the Park Hall accident three years earlier.

David Davies, the Cambrian chairman, and Mr Kendrick Minshall, the company solicitor, were present throughout the proceedings. Major Davies said early on, 'that the Cambrian desired, I may say more – demands – the most searching inquiry into the cause of the disaster'.

Mr Minshall intimated that probably ten witnesses connected with the company would be called, and said he hoped the proceedings could be completed in a day. The coroner expressed a doubt as to whether that could be done.

The magistrates bench of the court room was allocated to members of the press who had come from London, Yorkshire, Cardiff, Manchester, Birmingham and many other parts of the country, such was the interest in the accident.

Francis Thompson and John Parry were represented by Mr R.E. (Dicky) George, a solicitor from Newtown, on behalf of the Railway Clerks Union. William Jones, Frank Lewis and Ernest Rogers were represented by Mr J.H. (Jimmy) Thomas MP, general secretary of the NUR on behalf of the Amalgamated Society of Railway Servants.

Thomas was an ex-Great Western goods guard who finished his working life as colonial secretary in the Baldwin government. Even at that stage in his career at which we come across him, he was not a force to be trifled with; Thomas subjected both the Cambrian management and his own members to a severe grilling.

He started by expressing his personal sympathy for all those affected by the accident. He said that he quite understood what a delicate and responsible task the coroner and jury were called upon to face and while it would be his duty to protect the interests of the members of the union he represented, he would do so having regard to the public interest. It might be that they would profit from their experience of the sad occurrence. Mr Thomas felt he ought to say that Cambrian Railways had placed every facility at his disposal and he thanked them for the frank and open way in which they had assisted him materially.

Mr Farrell appeared for Tyers with a watching brief. Whilst the Tyer Co. was proud of its safety record, and confident that it was not implicated in the event, any adverse comment on the security of its system could have been very damaging. Tyer himself had died in 1912; his apparatus

The company chairman, Major David Davies.

having had an unblemished record up to that point. The express driver and firemen were not present at the inquest because of their ill-health, but had given statements.

Mr Thomas asked the coroner why the driver and fireman of the 'local' were not to be considered as contributory factors to the accident. The coroner ruled that as they had died in the crash, and the incident was almost certainly caused in the first instance by the station staff, the proceedings would not be investigating the crew's involvement. Confusingly, he also said that: 'If there was any negligence on the part of the poor driver and stoker, it does not absolve them that they are not here. If several persons are concerned with the negligence, they are all guilty.'

Colonel Pringle strongly made that point in his published report: 'ultimate responsibility for leaving a tablet station with the tablet for the section of the line over which he is about to run is laid upon the engine-driver.'

Apparently the Cambrian tried to make sure that its employees were 'singing from the same hymn sheet', as it summoned all concerned in the events to a meeting at company headquarters. It cannot be determined if this meeting was held before the inquiry or the subsequent inquest.

One modern commentator on the Cambrian writes. 'During a visit to the area, as recently as 1998, it was gleaned that perhaps not all the facts emerged during the inquiry.' It has been mentioned to the present author by a local source that it was a common practice for members of the station staff to be in the bar of the Abermule Hotel near the station yard. Keeping an

Company worthies seen at the last meeting before the Cambrian became part of the Great Western Railway. Standing, left to right: L. Colclough (works manager); J. Williamson (assistant engineer); S.G. Voles (assistant secretary); J. Burgess (assistant to the general manager); T.C. Sellars (assistant to the general manager). Seated: W. Finchett (goods manager); R. Williamson (accountant); G.C. McDonald (engineer and locomotive superintendent); S. Williamson (secretary and general manager); W.K. Minshall (solicitor); T.S. Goldsworthy (storekeeper); H. Warwick (superintendent of the line).

eye open for trains pulling up at the closed crossing gates, they would then run out, open the gates and carry on business as normal. Presumably this was only with goods trains as there would be less likelihood of there being any senior operating staff on board to question this unusual practice.

Colonel Pringle had held the official investigations for his inquiry on Saturday 29 January after he had visited the site of the crash by special train, departing from Oswestry at 8.45 a.m. He had been accompanied by Mr S. Williamson, the general manager; Mr G. MacDonald, the chief engineer and locomotive superintendent; Mr James Williamson, the assistant engineer; Mr H. Warwick, the traffic superintendent, and Mr W. Minshall, the company solicitor.

The press were waiting for them on their return at 11.45 a.m., but were disappointed as Colonel Pringle told them that he had decided to hold a closed inquiry as it was possible 'that several railwaymen's conduct might have to be investigated in a court of justice'. After taking various other depositions, as well as attending the inquest, he published his findings on 8 April 1921.

The Times in its leader of 31 January was scathing of Pringle's decision to hold his inquiry in private. Even after the terrible Quintinshill disaster, near Gretna in 1915, the investigation into the death of 214 Royal Scots aboard a troop train during wartime was held in public in spite of being a wonderful gift to the German propaganda machine.

Colonel Pringle had also conducted the Aisgill inquiry in 1913 when fourteen people were killed. On this occasion, the inquiry was held behind closed doors for the first day, then it was

The tempting watering holes in Abermule. The Waterloo Arms is on the right and the Abermule Hotel is just past it; they are equidistant from the station.

Engineer's inspection train headboard.

opened up to the public because of the strong protests which were made. *The Times*, 'did not recall that at the subsequent trial, any interests of justice had been prejudiced by the publicity given to the inquiry'.

An inquiry was not a Court of Justice; the Parliamentary Act of 1871, 34 & 35, Vic. Cap. 78, section 7, says: 'that the Board of Trade may direct an inquiry to be made by an inspecting officer into the cause of the accident.' The object of the inquiry was to determine the cause of an accident and what steps should be taken to prevent similar mishaps; it was not for the purposes of allocating blame. The men involved knew that whatever they said could not be used in evidence against them and so were more likely to speak freely. Only when there were fatalities and a criminal charge was therefore possible, did the question arise of whether or not to hold the inquiry in private. Where more than one person was involved, the difficulty of the decision was increased.

The inquest lasted for a day and a half of evidence taking. The atmosphere in the room must have been very intense and emotional, and surely no one would have envied the coroner his job.

The point was made during the proceedings that both Jones and Lewis had good records of service with the Cambrian. The company, however, had a long memory and comprehensive records; each man had been involved in separate minor incidents. Jones, for instance, had once been reprimanded for damaging a set of points, and Lewis, back in 1906, had accepted a consignment of sheep for transport without obtaining the necessary declaration from their putative owner. The driver and fireman of the 'local' had clean records.

The superintendent of the line, Henry Warwick, was cross-examined at length by Colonel Pringle and the coroner on the workings of the electric-tablet system. He produced the tablets in question, and used large photographs of the instruments to illustrate his explanation. The Train Registers were examined in detail; often there were no signatures, and the ownership of an entry had to be deduced from the handwriting. There was also lengthy discussion regarding the illegal operations at the station by the youngsters, and the lack of supervision and communication in general, both at Abermule and on the Cambrian.

As Lewis was about to give evidence, he was told by the coroner that he did not have to say anything, but he said that he would. When he came to answer questions about the departure of the 'down' train, he kept wiping tears away.

The coroner, in the course of the summing up which lasted forty-five minutes, emphasised that if the rules and regulations had been carried out there should have been no risk. He wanted the jury to note that some of the evidence which they had heard was contradictory; they would also have to consider whether there was any slackness on the part of the management which contributed to the accident.

The suggestion had been made rather forcibly during the receiving of evidence that it would be much safer and would prevent the division of responsibility if the tablet instruments were housed in the signal boxes. Surprisingly, it was claimed that that suggestion had never been put before the company.

The system in operation on the Cambrian was used on many other railways including most of those in the Scottish Highlands and on the single lines of the LNWR. The Ministry of Transport had so far not seen any reason why the tablet machines had to be kept in the signal box.

Colonel Pringle remarked it would be his duty to report to the Ministry what, if any, steps should be taken to prevent such a terrible disaster from happening again, and it was open to the jury to make any recommendation that it thought suitable.

He said that he had never known of a more remarkable set of circumstances than on this occasion. Everybody seemed to have assumed that everybody else knew what they knew. 'It seems to me gentlemen,' added the coroner, 'that if there are any evil spirits of carelessness, irresponsibility, and destruction they must have been hovering over Abermule Station at mid-day on 26 January.'

The coroner reminded the jury that part of its duty was to decide whether those men involved at Abermule on that fateful day were criminally responsible for the death of the seventeen people. He defined this responsibility:

> The person upon whom the law imposes any duty, or who has taken upon himself the duty of attending to the preservation of life, if he grossly neglects to perform that duty, or performs it with gross negligence and thereby causes the death of any person is guilty of manslaughter. As to what amount of negligence is to be regarded as gross, it is for you to consider.

He posed a number of questions which the jury needed to answer. The jury, composed of Newtown men, retired at 4.20 p.m. and was away from the court for about fifty minutes. Upon its return, the Foreman Mr T.L. Jones, a local wool merchant, answered the questions put by the coroner; he asserted that the answers had been arrived at unanimously.

The Questions

Were the deceased persons killed, or did they die of injuries, as a result of a collision between two trains?
Verdict: Yes.

What was the cause of the collision?
Verdict: By the issuing of the wrong tablet to the *'down'* train.

Was acting-stationmaster Lewis, the signalman, porter or clerk, guilty of gross negligence, or neglect in the performance of their duties that day as to the working of the tablet system, signalling, or in any other work?
Verdict: The acting-stationmaster Lewis and signalman Jones were guilty of gross neglect, and porter Rogers and clerk Thompson were guilty of negligence and excess of duty.

If so, was that gross negligence the direct and immediate course of the collision and resulting deaths?
Verdict: Yes.

Do the superior officers, including the stationmasters of the company, take reasonable precautions to see to the proper working of the rules and regulations as to the tablet system?
Verdict: We find that there has been a lack of supervision in carrying out the working of the tablet system.

Do you wish to make any recommendations to ensure the greater safety of the travelling public?
We recommend, (1) that the tablet system be worked from the signal box, (2) that stations on both sides of level-crossings should be connected by telephone on both sides.

The Verdict

ntering the
ny's Service.

Occupatic

Date.

Day.	Year.
16	1919

Jno. Cler

or Wages.

Per Annum.

13

The next stage of the proceedings is best recorded by the account in the *Montgomeryshire Advertiser*'s special edition of Thursday 3 February 1921. Unfortunately, the press report can give no impression of the intonation or body language of the participants during the various exchanges.

The coroner said to the foreman of the jury: 'You say as regards Lewis and Jones that they were guilty of gross neglect of their duty and that was the direct and immediate course of the accident.'

Foreman: 'Yes.'
Coroner: 'Therefore you say they are guilty of manslaughter?'
Foreman: 'Well that is the result of the finding.'
Coroner: 'It is a verdict of manslaughter against these two.' (Lewis and Jones)
Mr Thomas (representing Jones, Lewis and Rogers): 'Is it a verdict of manslaughter?'
Coroner: 'I think so.'
Mr Thomas: 'I respectfully suggest it is for the jury to say if it is manslaughter.'
Mr George (representing Thompson and Parry): 'I think too, they have not given that.'
Foreman: 'We find that in the discharge of their duty on this particular day they were guilty of gross neglect.'
Coroner: 'Then the result of that finding is a verdict of manslaughter.'
Mr Thomas:

> This is a grave matter and I am sure that you as coroner are anxious to do the right thing. I suggest it is too important for any one juryman to say it is a verdict of manslaughter. He is merely answering a question and it should come from the whole jury. Although they find the men guilty of gross neglect it may not warrant them in returning a verdict of manslaughter.

Coroner: 'They will have to say it is manslaughter before I put it down on the verdict.'
Foreman: 'I believe I shall be voicing the feeling of the jury in saying that the reason we were so long away was that we were considering this point most carefully. We all considered that our finding would result in a charge of manslaughter.'

We cannot be certain if Thomas was genuinely trying to seek clarification on the implied verdict of manslaughter, or whether he was trying to browbeat a provincial coroner and jury into returning a less damning verdict. The jury had accepted the fact that its verdict would result in a manslaughter charge, but was not prepared to voice the word.

The coroner, after further remarks by Mr Thomas, which were unreported, asked the jury if they would like to retire to reconsider their verdict. This time they were absent for about thirty minutes.

In reply to the coroner's question, 'Do you say that Lewis and Jones were guilty of gross negligence?', the foreman gave the reply: 'We have reconsidered it and we find, and it is unanimous, that Lewis and Jones were guilty of great neglect, and that calls for very severe censure.'

Coroner: 'Not manslaughter.'

The eloquent Mr Thomas had put the jury into a position where it actually had to use the word 'manslaughter', with all that implied, or return a lesser verdict.

The leader article in the next *Montgomeryshire Advertiser* was amazed at such a change of result:

> We cannot recall such an astounding incident in the history of jury service. Whether this altered view is right or wrong is not ours to declare, though it confounds the average imagination to try to reconcile the two pronouncements. There was the clear conviction in the mind of the jury that 'gross neglect' involved the arraignment of these two officials on a charge of manslaughter. Why, but a few minutes later was this judgement so altered as to place them without the pale of criminal culpability? A 'gross neglect', at the very least a 'great neglect', which accounted for the death of seventeen persons and the cruel suffering of many more, is considered to call only 'for the most severe censure.' Truly this is remarkable!

However incensed the *Montgomeryshire Advertiser*'s lead writer might have been, the verdict revolved around the coroner's advice to the jury before he sent them out: 'As to what amount of negligence is to be regarded as gross, it is for you to consider.'

After framing a verdict embracing the replies to the questions, the coroner called forward Lewis and Jones, who had been sitting at the back of the court, 'showing signs of great emotion'. The coroner addressed them in tones that were not clearly audible to the press. However, it is understood that he said he was glad that the jury had not found them guilty of the more serious form of neglect, under which charge he would have had to commit them to trial for manslaughter. The jury had found that the terrible collision was brought about by a great neglect on their part and that they were worthy of, and ought to have, severe censure. That he had to give, but he felt that they had been punished very severely by the agony of mind that they must have been in to think that they had contributed to the fearful accident. 'Both men appeared to feel their position acutely and tears streamed down their cheeks.'

On previous occasions, signalmen had been convicted of manslaughter, but had been discharged. For example, Signalman Holmes at Thirsk caused an express travelling at 60mph to crash into a stationary goods train; eight passengers were killed, and thirty-nine people injured. Holmes was charged with manslaughter and found guilty, but was absolutely discharged, a decision strongly supported by the jury and by public opinion. His young son had died during the previous night but he had still been required to man his watch in the signal box.

Signalmen Meakin and Tinsley, jointly responsible for the Quintinshill disaster, were the only signalmen in the United Kingdom to be given prison sentences for causing a railway accident; both were charged with 'neglect of duty'. Tinsley was jailed for three years, and Meakin for eighteen months, but both were released early.

Apparently, a feeling of distrust grew amongst some of the local railway workers, especially those of the NUR, because Jimmy Thomas had been seen at Cambrian Railways' headquarters having lunch with company board members. There is no record of whether this event took place before or after the inquest. With hindsight, it is hard to see how his conduct at the trial was anything other than beneficial to the staff involved.

Aftermath

Through its solicitor, Mr Minshall, the Cambrian Railways admitted its liability to pay compensation to the families of the dead and the injured.

This was not straightforward, and Mr Minshall had the parameters set down in writing for the board's perusal by 9 February. With regards to the persons who were killed, compensation was only payable to the wife, husband, parent or child, and was in proportion to the pecuniary loss sustained by the death. No damages were payable as a 'solatium or for funeral or mourning expenses'. The compensation payable to the company's servants was fixed in accordance with the Workman's Compensation Act and was limited to £300.

With regard to the persons injured, compensation was payable for actual pain or suffering, for the expense consequent upon the injury, and for pecuniary loss.

The Cambrian was insured with the Passengers' Assurance Co. up to a limit of £12,000; should the total rise above this amount, the assurance company would pay the total to the Cambrian and: 'leave them to deal with the claimants'.

Compensation first became available in England from 1849 when the Railway Passengers Assurance Co. of London was the first to provide personal cover against railway accidents. This was a recognition of increasing public concern over railway safety. However, the railway companies' booking clerks, who sold the insurance to travellers when they bought tickets, were instructed by their employers not to invite the taking of insurance directly. This was for fear that 'open discussion of potential disasters on the railway might increase anxiety among travellers'!

By 6 April, Mr Kendrick reported that eleven death claims had been made, but only two had been settled. *The Times* of 31 October noted that Mrs Clara Elizabeth Slade, whose husband was killed in the crash, had only just been awarded £1,300 by Mr Justice McCardie at Chester Assizes.

Reginald Ernest Daines, an insurance official of Wrexham, claimed damages for personal injuries and was awarded £425 with costs. Mr Kendrick said at this time that there had been fifty-eight claims as a result of the accident and only eight had not been settled amicably.

In the case of death, a number of claimants, such as the relatives of Miss Scott Owen, a gifted artist, and the parents of the Onslow boys, felt that the 'pecuniary loss' calculation ought to be improved upon by an 'incidental loss' addition. The chairman of the Cambrian agreed to an extra ex-gratia amount, unspecified in the documents.

The compensation of £300 each had been paid into court for the driver and the guard, but the fireman had no dependant relatives; the board finally paid out the princely sum of £34 4s 0d to his family in November.

The four men most closely involved in the events did not remain long in the company's employment. When a reporter went to the station the following day, they were no longer there; presumably stationmaster Parry was back in charge after having been recalled from his holiday.

It was resolved at a meeting of the Traffic & Works Committee held at the Great Western Railway's Royal Hotel at Paddington on 16 February, that 'the services of the men be dispensed with'. Parry's fate was still under discussion; it appears as if he retained his position. The nephew of the express driver met him in the late 1930s at Cemaes Road.

Name.	Age last birthday.	Place.	Grade.	Date.	Date resumed.	Nature of Injury.	Weekly Compensation Payable.
							£. s. d.
E.A.Evans.	17.	Oswestry.	Cleaner.	Jan. 5.	Jan.17.	Wrist burnt.	1.10. 0.
J.E.Hampson.	44.	Abermule.	Fitter.	Jan.28.	Still off.	Wrist crushed.	1.15. 0.
.Jones.	67.	Abermule.	Driver.	Jan.26.		Fatally injured in Abermule accident.	
E.W.Evans.	25.	Abermule.	Fireman.	Jan.26.		Fatally injured in Abermule accident.	
J.P.Jones.	45.	Abermule.	Driver.	Jan.26.	Still off.	Injured in Abermule accident.	
.Owen.	42.	Abermule.	Fireman.	Jan.26.	Still off.	"	" " "
E.Humphreys.	43.	Abermule.	Driver.	Jan.26.	Still off.	"	" " "
W.S.Edwards.	24.	Abermule.	Fireman.	Jan.26.	Still off.	"	" " "

I am,

MY LORDS and GENTLEMEN,

Yours faithfully,

geu Donald.

The problem of compensation…

As an employer, the Cambrian Railways was typical of its era. The company did alleviate a great deal of unemployment, especially in rural areas, and acted as a much-needed check to depopulation. It was, however, able to dictate pay, and conditions and terms of service. Staff often had to work up to thirty-six hours of continuous duty. Discipline was strict – for example, all staff had to carry a copy of the rules and regulations. If they were caught without it the fine was five shillings, a significant sum. A stationmaster would face dismissal for failing to send in his accounts on time, and a clerk had been dismissed for 'interfering with' a tablet instrument. On one occasion, a driver who had over-run a station, therefore technically entering the next section without the correct tablet, was suspended for three weeks and demoted to the lowest grade. The stationmaster involved, who could have done nothing to prevent the incident, was dismissed.

| NAME (in full) | | | | Francis Wm. Thompson. | | | | | |

On entering the Company's Service. Date.	Occupation.	STATION.	Salary or Wages Advanced.					OFI
			Date.	Per Week.	Per Annum	Date.	Nature of OI

Month.	Day.	Year.			
June	16	1919	Jas. Clerk	Abermule	Oct 15/19 · 5/9 · 15 · ·
					Ap.e 6/20 · 13/5 · 35 ·

Salary or Wages.	
Per Week.	Per Annum.
5 ·	13 · ·

(?) Dismissed in connection with Abermule Accident 25/2/21

Date of Birth.		
Month.	Day.	Year.
Ap.e	6	1905

'Their services be dispensed with…'

The enginemen of the express, driver John Pritchard Jones and fireman Bert Owen, were both off duty on full wages for almost a year. In the June following they were still attending hospital daily for treatment. They were each granted a bonus of £5 by the Cambrian Railways board. Eventually they resumed duties, but 'kept seeing things coming at them round curves'. Pritchard Jones's great nephew believes that he never drove on the main line again. He later became charge hand of the Locomotive Department at Aberystwyth; he died in August 1944.

Pritchard Jones had not been rostered to drive the express that day, but had changed turns at the last minute with Driver Lewis Rees.

One source reckons that Owen, a passed-fireman, was promoted to driver shortly after the accident, but this has not been confirmed. His daughter recalled that he never spoke about the event, but suffered from mental problems for the rest of his life. His wife often had to calm him down during the night. By the 1930s he was living with his wife and daughter in Aberystwyth; he was a very keen gardener, but had become very reclusive and hardly spoke to anyone. He became the caretaker of the local Welsh Methodist church in Queen's Road.

Porter Ernie Rogers left the Cambrian's employment on 28 February, but was later offered his job back when the company became part of the Great Western Railway under the 1922 grouping. He did not take up the offer, but found employment at Boys & Bowden in Welshpool, then later as a builder working with his, by now, brothers-in-law. He rarely spoke about the incident, but did say on one occasion that supervision at the station was nonsense. However, the staff would soon be in trouble if they did not keep the traffic moving.

He accidentally met up with Frank Lewis years later, and Frank said to him, 'I'm sorry Ernie, I wish I'd taken the rap for that. I'd have felt a better man.'

Shortly after the crash, two Swindon-built outside-framed ex-GWR 4-4-0 locomotives were bought off the Bute Dock Supply Co. as replacement engines. Rather insensitively, the Cambrian allotted them numbers 85 and 92, though they never carried them; they retained their old numbers of 3521 and 3546.

Although they were not a contributory factor to the disaster, the Abermule crossing gates were modified so that they could be locked from the signal box at a cost of £70.

Quite apart from the seriousness of the Abermule collision in itself, the general practice of single-line working came under more than usually detailed scrutiny. Even though the equipment was not to blame, the accident had sent shivers down the spines of the numerous companies who operated single-line working under Tyer or similar systems, such as the LNWR's Webb & Thompson apparatus.

The ripples spread far afield. For many years afterwards, operating departments of the mainly single-track Indian Railways, in which British staff were heavily involved, displayed notices which warned: 'Remember Abermule.' A local man remembers that his father, along with a number of friends, left the employment backwater that was Abermule in the early 1920s by enlisting in the Army. After a long boat voyage, they landed in India, marched through the docks to the railway station and were greeted by those very same notices. It seemed an omen to them.

The author recently heard from a young man who used to while away his spare time in the signal box at Borth in the 1930s. He recalled one day that he offered to take the tablet out of the instrument; the signalman glared at him and said: 'Remember Abermule'.

However, Abermule was not the first warning that humans could overcome the apparently foolproof technology for protecting the Cambrian Railways' single lines. Just over three years earlier a very serious, but little known, accident had occurred at Park Hall, near Oswestry, near to the present-day orthopaedic hospital. Two goods trains met in head-on collision. This was the accident that Ewart Thomas had survived, depsite being thrown out of his van.

Park Hall, on the Gobowen branch, had been one of the biggest army bases and PoW compounds in Britain during the First World War – it was still a major source of traffic for many years after the cessation of hostilities. The inquiry revealed the startling fact that two correct tablets had been issued for the same section, but for opposing trains. The instruments in question were of the 'less electrically robust' McKenzie & Holland manufacture, not Tyer's.

The full details of how it happened were never fully established; the men involved told conflicting stories about an apparently impossible happening. Because of very severe snow conditions, some of the instrument wires had shorted and no tablets could be removed as long as the fault remained. This in itself was a vindication of the apparatus. However, the signalmen had apparently found a way to bypass the system by connecting it electrically to the railway telegraph machines; unfortunately they had not coordinated their attempts to keep the traffic running. Only the fact that no passenger train was involved, and there was only one death, that of fireman Thomas Dyke, allowed the accident to pass almost unnoticed by the general public. Once again the accident was inadvertently caused by company employees attempting to keep the railway running as efficiently as possible.

Scrutiny of the Board of Trade accident returns reveals remarkably few incidents notified by the Cambrian compared with other lines of similar size; whether this was because they did not occur, or because they were not always notified to the authorities, remains open to conjecture. Certainly in the early days when Cambrian trains came to grief they were never going very fast, and by the nature of their traffic working, it was often the rolling stock of other companies which came to grief.

In the case of Abermule there was no suggestion that the physical working of the tablet instruments was incorrect – it was the practices surrounding the block working that failed so disastrously. Sir John Pringle felt:

> So strongly that due regard will in future be paid by all concerned to the rules and regulations for single line working, by which so high a degree of security has been obtained in the past upon British railways, that it is difficult to find justification for calling for the provision of additional precautions at all single line tablet or staff posts.

However, he did recommend that there should be electric interlocking between the tablet instruments and the starting signal leading into a single-line section. This would make it impossible to clear the signal unless a token had been withdrawn from the correct instrument for the section that was being entered.

Colonel Pringle had also recommended that as:

It is now permissible to work those points [west-end loop points at Abermule] direct from the signal box, simplification of working will result from doing away with the ground-frame, and action in this direction by the company is not only desirable, but necessary…

It had in fact been permissible since Board of Trade regulations had been relaxed to allow a distance of 200 yards around the turn of the century. The Cambrian had not taken advantage of this.

According to the magazine *Travel and Transport Monthly* of April 1922, the Cambrian had spent £480 on the provision of extension bells on tablet instruments. During the following twelve months, £4,500 was to be allocated in continuing this work and in interlocking tablet instruments with the signals.

Commemoration

In the spirit of wordsmiths such as the poet McGonagall, who immortalised the Tay Bridge disaster of 1879, and Denis Muir who wrote of Quintinshill, a local man, Mr Evan Andrew of Tregynon, wrote a set of heroic verses, under the Welsh pen-name Ap Maldwyn, about the disaster at Red House Farm.

He and his family were moving house on that day from Bwlchyffridd to Abermule, passing right by the crash site. The recitation of his work in the parlour, at social gatherings, and even at the Eisteddfod, was a popular pastime in mid-Wales during the following months and years:

One January morning, the sixth and twentieth day
What happened on the Cambrian, I'll show in mournful lay
It was as fair a morning as winter could produce
When the Express as usual came out for travellers' use
From Aberystwyth station, soon after ten o'clock
it sped by shade and hillside and many a rugged rock
Some half a dozen coaches the mighty engine drew
from station unto station in eager haste it flew
The track was well attended, each man stood at his post
obstructions were prevented that time might not be lost
No 'danger signal' beckon'd, free course was to be seen
The driver fear'd no evil, in station nor between
Of dread, ill-fate and danger the thought had not been born
in passenger nor driver, upon that peaceful morn
It left the Vale of Dovey, and climb'd Talerddig hill
And hurried for the Severn and dashed o'er many a rill
Through village, town and hamlet, it sped upon its way
and nothing yet predicted its awful doom that day
The passengers seem'd happy, some chatted with content
some read the daily papers, on sleeping some were bent
The fireman and the driver they watched the line ahead
and Oh! they spied an engine, towards their own it sped
They turn'd off steam and whistl'd and quickly press'd the brake
And shouted in their panic 'a leap for life we'll take'
No sooner had they ventured to take their daring dash
when there, and in an instant, they heard the mighty crash
Like thunderbolts terrific the steaming engines met
and in one heap of ruins together both were set
Out bursting from its chambers the wild steam hiss'd aloud
and leap'd in curling volumes which formed a dreadful cloud
That cloud was quickly vanish'd And O! the awful sight
the coaches jamm'd in matchwood, death reign'd on left and right

Appalling was that picture, the dead in silence lay
Conceal'd within the wreckage their pain had passed away
Twas sad indeed to witness the moaning injured there
'twas like a scene of battle – a scene of deep despair
A host of eager helpers flew to that dismal spot
where sorrow and bereavement became their woeful lot

Survivors of the wreckage made haste to ascertain
what of their dearest lov'd ones, who travelled on that train
Alas! their hopes were shattered their hearts with sorrow fill'd
when there they found their dear ones were number'd with the kill'd
So bitter was the trial, that mourners sobb'd aloud
to find their friends encircl'd with matchwood for a shroud
Twas voic'd in every region, that woeful sad event
with gloom the tale were utter'd in tears of deep lament
Skilled nurses and physicians were quickly there to give
their service to the injured – the suffering to relieve
The names of sixteen victims on the death roll were found
Distressing was the story to all the country round
That God-sent Institution which stood not far away
threw wide its welcoming portals, Oh! what a boon that day!
Remedy for the injured and covert for the dead
were found within its precincts – a balm for those that bled
With grief 'twill be remembered that curve upon the line
the ties that there were sever'd will cause hearts to repine
Had someone made a blunder and overlooked a rule?
Why did that local engine, steam off from Abermule?
What caus'd the grave disaster that noonday on the curve?
And does the 'tablet system' for safety, stand to serve?
Alas! our little queries will only be in vain
and seeking explanations will only deepen pain
Inevitable turnings we meet in nature's realm
And systems prove a failure while man is at the helm

There is also a tale of a ghostly spectre attached to the accident. Henry Stanhope wrote the following story in *The Times*, of 3 July 1987 in his article 'Unidentified Sighing Object':

My father always wondered if he had seen a ghost following an experience in the winter of 1921 near his home outside the Welsh border town of Montgomery. Then still in his teens, he had gone to post a letter on Montgomery station, which was some distance from the town and had the only pillar box for miles.

He crunched his way back along an empty station path, his breath steaming in the crisp night air. As he reached for the gate at the end of the path he touched a gloved hand resting on it. He leapt back, startled, to find himself staring into the heavily veiled face of a woman dressed in black, who was standing in the shadows beside the hedge. 'Is there another train tonight?' she asked, and sighed as my father nervously replied. 'In two hour's time.'

'Oh, what a pity' she said, and with that, disappeared. My father reached for the gate, to find the hand had gone and no woman was standing there. Subsequent inquiries proved that she did not catch the train that night, or answer to the description of anyone who had been seen in the neighbourhood – where strangers were remarkable anyway. To his knowledge she never reappeared.

The primary school at Abermule staged a commemorative event in 1996, the seventy-fifth anniversary of the disaster. The pupils re-enacted the events leading up to the accident under the guidance of Terry Wain, the headteacher. The school event attracted a lot of publicity and Mr Wain kept a log book of the phone calls which the school received offering information. The drama also appeared in S4C's *Fishlock's Wild Tracks*, and triggered a Welsh language programme on S4C which re-constructed the event – this was presented by Gwyn Briwnant-Jones, the Welsh railway historian and artist. The school was awarded a major and prestigious educational prize for its efforts.

Many local people loaned items for the display which accompanied the drama and Mr Wain joked to the author that if many more artefacts had been unearthed, they could have re-created the wreck site. They had the whistle which sent the express train on its way from Newtown, though there are at least two whistles which lay claim to this honour! There was a damaged buffer which had lain ever since in someone's rockery and there was part of a carriage door. The remains of the oxyacetylene set which was used to cut up the wreckage also made an appearance.

The Cambrian Railway's museum at Oswestry contains a number of relics, including plaques commemorating the event; these are made from the wood of the wrecked vehicles, and usually carry the carriage number. There are also others in private hands, but the Ceredigion Museum at Aberystwyth can go one better - it holds the 'Abermule triptych'.

Three postcard-sized photographs of the crash scene are mounted in a frame (10 x 47 cms). Originally, the frame, dated Paddington, 1903, was probably a warning sign about using the communication cord, and not throwing bottles out of the window, and a list of places at which baskets of hot meals were available.

The triptych consists of a thick piece of oak with the frame screwed (twelve brass screws), nailed and partly glued in place. Underneath the pictures the initials LW and the number 1,155 are written in pencil. On the back are stamped '11' and '7730'. GWR coach No.7730 was the Aberystwyth to Paddington coach with brake compartment which suffered the majority of the damage.

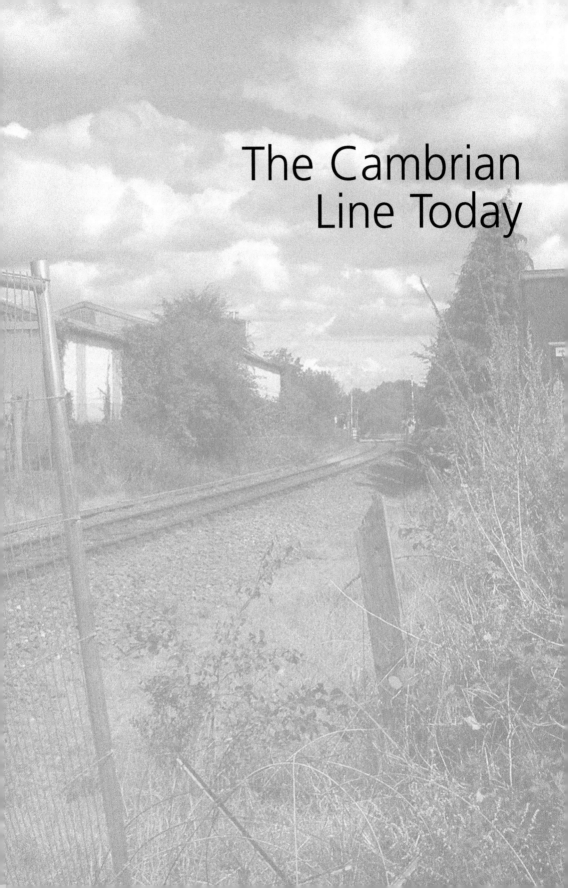

The Cambrian Line Today

In the years that have gone by since the Abermule disaster there has been no single-line collision of this nature on any British railway, and there is good reason to hope that there never will be another. There are only three single-line sections in the country still worked by the antiquated Tyer's electric tablet instruments, as well as perhaps a preserved line or two.

At the remote station of Barrhill, on the Glasgow to Stranraer single-line route, the signal box remains in use to control a passing loop, and believe it or not, the instruments are housed in the booking office to allow the signalman to also carry out other duties.

The present day 'tablet' system on the old Cambrian main line is the Radio Electronic Token Block, RETB – it was brought into use in October 1988. The 135 miles from Shrewsbury to Aberystwyth and Pwllheli are now divided into fourteen sections, centrally controlled at Machynlleth box by two men using two computer desks, and the original fifty-lever frame that has been retained to work the Dovey Junction section via TCB signalling. No one has to leave either cab or signal box to hand over a tablet, and hopefully all possibilities of human failing have been removed from the system.

If plans had gone ahead in the early 1860s, Cilgwrgan would have been a junction for the branch to Tregynon. Cutting through Aber Bechan, it was planned to follow closely the line of the B4369 to Bettws Cedewain and then ramble alongside the Bechain Brook (B4389) to Tregynon. However, it remained as a proposal only; some say that it was never more than a possible status symbol for the Hanbury-Stacy family of Gregynog.

The lady crossing keeper at Cilgwrgan was killed in an unexplained accident in September 1964. A major review of the safety of level-crossings in mid-Wales was carried out by Network Rail, following the death of Kathleen Yettman, from Ohio, at Llanbrynmair crossing on 29 October 1999. An inquest returned a verdict of accidental death after the car in which she was travelling was struck by a train on the unmanned level-crossing. The vehicle was catapulted 50 yards along the track by the 60mph collision with the Lincoln to Aberystwyth passenger train.

Local residents said they had complained regularly about the warning lights, yet the gates on the crossing were often left open... by the local residents. At the end of 2005, Cilgwrgan crossing was closed and the road re-routed, in a scheme costing over £3 million.

Dr Richard Beeching's report on 'The Shaping of Britain's Railways' was issued on 27 March 1963. Nearly a third of the country's passenger stations and halts were recommended for closure in the next few years; it came as little surprise that Abermule was included in the list. There was a local attempt to have the signal box 'listed' but unfortunately that came to nothing.

However much, or little, times have changed on Britain's rail transport system, for anyone interested in or connected with railways, the name of that quiet little Welsh country station, 'Abermule Change for Kerry', will always carry sinister and tragic overtones of human nature abusing a system designed to run a railway in complete safety.

Machynlleth signal box in the early twenty-first century.

Machynlleth signal box in the early twenty-first century.

Abermule today, looking towards Montgomery from the Kerry sidings.

Bibliography

Cambrian Railways

Briwnant-Jones, Gwyn (1999), *Talerddig in Great Western Days*, Gomer Press
Christiansen, Rex, Miller, R.W (1968 & 1971), *The Cambrian Railways*, David and Charles
Christiansen, Rex (1999), *The Cambrian Railways; Portrait of a Welsh Railway Network*, Ian Allan
    Publishing
Dalton, T.P. (1985), *Cambrian Companionship*, OPC Print
Kinder, R.W. (1982), *The Cambrian Railways*, Oakwood Press
www.nationalarchives.gov.uk Rail 92/17; Rail 92/96; Rail 92/125; Rail 1057
Railway Staff Registers; Cheshire County Archives NPR/26; NPR/27

The Accident

Blythe, R. (1951), *Danger Ahead*, Newman Neane
Eds (2000), *British Railway Disasters*, Eds. Ian Allan Publishing
Hamilton, J.A.B. (1967), *British Railway Accidents of the Twentieth Century*, George Allen &
    Unwin
Jones, Elwyn V. (2003), *Mishaps on the Cambrian Railway*, Private Publishing (Cambrian Railway
    Society)
Nock, O.S. (1970), *Historic Railway Disasters*, Arrow
Pringle, J (Col.). Director General, Public Safety & General Purposes Department, *Ministry of
    Transport Inquiry into the Collision at Abermule*, 8 April 1921.
Rolt, L.T.C. (1966), *Red for Danger*, Pan
Vaughan, Adrian (1989), *Obstruction Danger*, Patrick Stephens

Signalling

Stirling, D. (1991), *Electric Token Block Instruments*; Signalling Paper No.11, Signalling Record
    Society
Vanns, Michael A. (1995), *Signalling in the Age of Steam*, Ian Allan Publishing
www.signalbox.org
www.railwaysarchive.co.uk

General

Cozens, L., Kinder, R.W., Poole, Brian (2001), *The Mawddwy, Van and Kerry Branches*, The Oakwood Press. Usk, Mons

Davies, David Wyn (1986), *A Welshman in Mesopotamia*, Gwasg Cambria, Aberystwyth

Davies, G.H. (repro.2000), *Old Railway Characters in mid-Wales*, Aberystwyth

Davies, J. (1991, repro.2000), *How I Became a Train Driver*, 'Abergynolwyn', Aberystwyth

Oppitz, Leslie (2004), *Lost Railways of Shropshire*, Countryside

Faith, Nicholas (1998), *Derail*, Channel4 Books, Macmillan

Gresham, Colin, A. (1983), *James Gresham and the Vacuum Railway Brake*, Cyhoeddiadau Mei. Penygroes, Caernarvon

Newspapers (British Library Newspapers, Colindale)

The Times
42,629	27 January 1921
42,630	28 January 1921
42,631	29 January 1921
42,632	31 January 1921
42,635	3 February 1921
42,636	4 February 1921

The Illustrated London News
5 February 1921, pp. 160, 164, 165

Daily Mirror
5,380	27 January 1921 pp 1 & 3
5,381	28 January 1921 pp 1 & 3
	1 February 1921
	3 February 1921

The Wheatsheaf, Co-op Society Journal
Feb, 1921

The Sphere
5 February 1921, pp.138, Supp. Vi

Travel and Transport Monthly
April 1922

Montgomery County Times and mid-Wales Advertiser
| 3,247 | 30 January 1921 pp. 3, 5, 8 |
| 3,248 | 5 February 1921 pp. 2, 5, 6, 8 |

Montgomeryshire Express and Radnor Times
| 3,024 | 29 January 1921, pp. 2, 3, 4, 5 |

Special Editions

            2 February 1921 (Wednesday)   pp. 1, 2 (Only available at Newtown Library)
            3 February 1921 (Thursday)   pp. 1, 2 (Only available at Newtown Library)
3,025   4 February 1921   pages 2, 3, 4 & 7

County Times
20 January 1971
27 January 1971
3 February 1971

Miscellaneous
The script of the Abermule Primary School drama.
Contacts log for the Primary School event.

Index

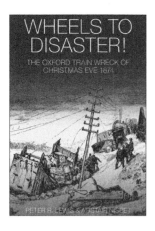

Other titles published by The History Press

Wheels to Disaster! The Oxford Train Wreck of 1874
PETER R. LEWIS & ALISTAIR NISBET

On Christmas Eve in 1874 the worst accident in the history of the GWR occurred at Shipton-on-Cherwell, several miles from Oxford, when the 10 a.m. from London Paddington to Birkenhead derailed, killing thirty-four passengers. The fracture of a single tyre was enough to cause this catastrophe due to the lack of continuous braking and inadequate communication between the driver and passengers.
978 07524 4512 0

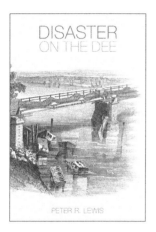

Disaster on the Dee
PETER R. LEWIS

The fall of the Dee bridge in May 1847 was one of the first major railway disasters in Britain. It occurred just outside Chester with the loss of five lives. The line and chief engineer Robert Stephenson were nationally slated and virtually accused of manslaughter when his cast-iron bridge failed so catastrophically.

Full of detailed technical insight and illustrated with a wealth of contemporary material, this informative book will be of great use for engineering students and historians and will also appeal to railway enthusiasts and interested locals.
978 07524 4266 2

Beautiful Railway Bridge of the Silvery Tay Reinvestigating the Tay Bridge Disaster of 1879
PETER R. LEWIS

125 years ago, barely a year and a half after the Tay Railway Bridge was built, William McGonnagal was composing his poem about the Tay Bridge disaster, the famous poem about Britain's worst ever engineering disaster. Over eighty people lost their lives in the incident, but how did it happen? The accident reports say it was high wind and poor construction, but Peter Lewis tells the real story of how the bridge so spectacularly collapsed on 28 December 1879.

978 07524 3160 4